A RESILIENT LIFE

YOU CAN MOVE AHEAD NO MATTER WHAT

GORDON MacDONALD

NELSON BOOKS
A Division of Thomas Nelson Publishers
Since 1798
www.thomasnelson.com

Copyright © 2004 by Gordon MacDonald

All rights reserved. No portion of this book may be reproduced, stored in a retrieval system, or transmitted in any form or by any means—electronic, mechanical, photocopy, recording, scanning, or other—except for brief quotations in critical reviews or articles, without the prior written permission of the publisher.

Published in Nashville, Tennessee, by Thomas Nelson, Inc.

Published in association with the literary agency of Wolgemuth & Associates, Inc.

Nelson Books titles may be purchased in bulk for educational, business, fundraising, or sales promotional use. For information, please email SpecialMarkets@ThomasNelson.com.

Unless otherwise indicated, Scripture taken from the *HOLY BIBLE, NEW INTERNATIONAL VERSION.* Copyright 1973, 1978, 1984 by International Bible Society. Used by permission of Zondervan Publishing House. All rights reserved.

Scriptures marked KJV are from the Holy Bible, King James Version.

Library of Congress Cataloging-in-Publication Data

MacDonald, Gordon, 1939-
    A resilient life : you can move ahead no matter what / Gordon MacDonald.
    p. cm.
Includes bibliographical references.
    ISBN 0-7852-7151-1 (hardcover)
    ISBN-10: 0-7852-8791-4 (tp)
    ISBN-13: 978-0-7852-8791-9 (tp)
    1. Resilience (Personality trait)—Religious aspects—Christianity. I. Title.
BV4597.58.R47M23 2004
248.4—dc22

                    2004024245

Printed in the United States of America

06 07 08 09 10 11 RRD 9 8 7 6 5 4

To Gail, now my wife of forty-four years (at this writing). She models all that I have learned about resilience. And I want the world to know how deep is my love and respect for her.

And with appreciation to Robert Wolgemuth (my literary representative), Victor Oliver (my long-time publisher) and Kristen Lucas (my editor) who have been my teammates in writing this book. Their encouragement has kept me going throughout this project

CONTENTS

I

RESILIENT PEOPLE ARE COMMITTED TO FINISHING STRONG

II

RESILIENT PEOPLE RUN INSPIRED BY A BIG-PICTURE VIEW OF LIFE

III

RESILIENT PEOPLE RUN FREE OF THE WEIGHT OF THE PAST

CONTENTS

IV
RESILIENT PEOPLE TRAIN TO GO THE DISTANCE

V
RESILIENT PEOPLE RUN IN THE COMPANY OF A "HAPPY FEW"

A NOTE FROM GORDON MACDONALD

In the great race of life, there are some Christ-followers who stand out from all the rest. I call them the resilient ones. The further they run, the stronger they get. They seem to possess these spiritual qualities:

> They are committed to finishing strong.
> They run inspired by a big-picture view of life.
> They run free of the weight of the past.
> They run confidently, trained to go the distance.
> They run in the company of a "happy few."

Writing to people whose suffering was so intense that they were in danger of losing confidence in God, the author of the book of Hebrews recalled the adventures of the great Biblical heroes—the men and women of unshakable faith: *the first resilient ones*. Then visualizing those champions as spectators at the games, he called his readers to the starting line of a great race.

> Since we are surrounded by such a great cloud of witnesses, let us throw off everything that hinders and the sin that so easily entangles, and let us run with . . .
>
> *resilience*
>
> . . . the race marked out for us. Let us fix our eyes on Jesus, the author and perfecter of our faith, who for the joy set

before him endured the cross, scorning its shame, and sat down at the right hand of the throne of God. Consider him who endured such opposition from sinful men, so that you will not grow weary and lose heart. (Heb. 12:1–3)

[And Simon Peter said to Jesus] *"Go away from me, Lord; I am a sinful man!"....[But] Jesus said to Simon, "Don't be afraid; from now on you will catch men."* *(Luke 5:8,10)*

———

THE WIMP

In the archives of my mind is a picture of a white bulletin board. It is, or rather *was*, a simple piece of plywood (two feet by five feet, maybe) nailed to two vertical four-by-four-foot posts. Embedded in its surface were perhaps a thousand spent staples, representing lots of pages that were at one time or another affixed to the board. This bulletin board was near the top of the turn in a dirt running track at the Stony Brook School, a college preparatory school located on the north shore of Long Island, New York.

The information pinned to the board each weekday at noon played an important part in my life for the three years that I was a Stony Brook student.

Some thought that the white board was the personal property of Marvin W. Goldberg (MWG was his familiar shorthand signature), Stony Brook's once-upon-a-time track and cross-country coach. I can see him now (and this is almost fifty years later) as he left his Hegeman Hall office—just before the lunchtime bell—and walked to the track. In one hand would be several sheets of paper. In the other, a stapler to tack the papers to the board.

On the papers, written in the blue ink that flowed from the broad point of Goldberg's fountain pen: individual programs for each member of his team—warm-ups, workouts, and technical development.

Athletes whose names, like mine, began with *M*, were usually on the third or fourth of the seven sheets that Goldberg would fasten to the white board. Curious, I would often trot down to the track as soon as the coach had gone his way to get a peek at what he'd planned for me to do that day.

If I could not get down to the white bulletin board myself, other teammates would. At lunch you would hear the trackmen talking among themselves: "You're not going to believe what Goldberg's got for you today!" or "Are *you* ever in deep trouble!" No one ever said, "What a wonderful afternoon we're going to have on the track! Goldberg's going to run our legs off, and I can't wait."

At three thirty the track team (or cross-country team, depending upon the season) began its workouts. First came the nonnegotiable warm-ups, then the workouts designed to build stamina and speed, and finally the technical work: perfecting length of stride, relay practice, discussion on race strategy, etc.

———

The workouts, each about two hours in length, were carefully planned by Coach Goldberg. They were not created on the spot. Everything was in alignment with a personal plan conceived for each athlete months (if not a year) before. If you had asked him why you were doing certain kinds of time trials on a snowy Thursday afternoon in January, he might say, "Reaching this goal now will make it possible for you to run a 400 meters in [here he would name a certain time] at the Penn Relays in late April." And then he'd add, "Everything we're doing today will have its payoff in late May. You'll see."

Baton exchanges between relay-team members were a good example of technical development: twenty-five minutes of top-speed baton handoffs. Exhausting! The coach repeatedly reminded relay-team members that close races were won or lost in the handoff box, and this justified striving to achieve perfect timing during the exchanges. Dropping a baton in one of those handoffs? Unthinkable! That could make Marvin Goldberg an unhappy man.

MWG was aware that some of us complained behind his back about the relentless practice of handoffs. "You'll be a part of relay teams all your life," he said to me one day. "If you have a family or if you work with people on a job, there will be those moments where you'll have to hand off an important message or an assignment to someone. It's in those handoffs throughout life where most mistakes happen and problems get started. So learn to do *these* kinds of hand-offs now, and you'll be ready for more important handoffs later on."

It took me years to appreciate the coach's larger view of what seemed to me as a teenager as little more than an exchange of a stick from one hand to another. But then Goldberg saw everything in terms of building people for the future; I couldn't see that far ahead.

I have often written and spoken of Marvin Goldberg and the remarkable impression he made on my teenage life. I saw him as a serious man who expected the best out of everyone. People who knew him would probably not say he had a great sense of humor, but they would certainly recall his passion for excellence and total effort. They would doubtless also remember his ambition to help young men (and later women, when Stony Brook turned co-educational) fulfill their human potential, and they would never forget his desire for all of his protégés to make lifelong obedience to God their highest aspiration.

I entered Stony Brook as a sophomore. I came with the intention to play football as a running back. I was driven by a fantasy of the day the football coach would present me with a large letter *S* at an athletic banquet. He would say, "And now a varsity letter to Stony Brook's greatest running back and this year's most valuable player . . ." The letter would be sewn to a white cardigan sweater, and, in the continuing fantasy, some pretty ponytailed girl would beg to wear it for an afternoon.

The major obstacle between me and that letter *S*, unfortunately, was that I was built like a toothpick. And that presented immediate problems in the first days of fall football practice. No one had informed me that I would be expected to crash into linemen who were considerably (and this is an understatement) bulkier than I was. No one mentioned that those behemoths loved causing pain. Since I wasn't attracted to bumps and bruises, my days as a football player came quickly to an end.

I've imagined a phone conversation between the football people and Coach Goldberg. "Marvin, we've got this kid over here. He's a bit of a wimp, frankly. Doesn't like getting creamed. But, hey, he's a fast wimp. You might want to take a look at him. We wish you'd do it quickly; we need his locker and his pads."

Whether it was because of this conversation or something similar, I was traded by the football coach to the track and cross-country coach *for nothing*. The next day I reported to the track in a bathing suit and high-top sneakers. Sleek, fast, highly conditioned runners already at the track snickered.

I spent my first days running time trials for Coach Goldberg. He would watch, then make a few suggestions about the motion of my arms or the angle of my head or the length of my stride. He offered few compliments, and his critiques were frequent. My self-confidence—already wounded on the football field—sagged even further, because the man gave no indications at all about his impressions of my running ability. Nothing! I began to doubt that I would ever earn the big Stony Brook *S*, either as a football player or as a runner. All Goldberg would say at the end of a practice was, "See you tomorrow." So I kept showing up.

Then one day, Goldberg called out to me just as I was finishing a set of sprints, "Gordie, come here, please." *Gordie*. The coach had given me a new name. The football coaches had simply called me MacDonald or Mac. But to Marvin Goldberg I became "Gordie" the first day I met him. It was a name I found I loved, and that—strange as it may seem—gave me a new view of myself. Gordon, I'd always felt, was an old man's name, and I'd never liked it. Had MWG intuited this? Today, as an older man, I am a Gordon again to all but my wife, who continues to call me Gordie, especially when she is greatly pleased with me. Her "Gordon!" is a storm signal.

Upon hearing my new name, I headed in Goldberg's direction. He was standing next to the white bulletin board. When I reached him, Goldberg put his hand on my shoulder and began to speak. As best as I can recall his words after all these years, he said, "Gordie, I've been watching you carefully. I think you have the potential to be an excellent runner. You have a runner's body and a natural stride. And you are fast. But you have much to learn. If you are to compete for Stony Brook, you're going to have to work hard. You'll have to learn to discipline yourself, and it will mean that you have to trust me and follow my instructions. Every day you will have to come to this track and complete the workouts that will be listed on this board. Now, Gordie [the coach repeated one's name often], don't commit to this if you are not willing to give it everything you have." And then he posed this question, "Gordie, are you willing to pay the price it takes to become a Stony Brook trackman?"

Looking back now with a bit more perspective, I realize how little idea I had of what the man was saying. I heard the words but understood little of their meaning. Trust him? Follow his instructions? Pay the price? No one had ever talked to me this way before! *Sure, why not?* I thought. *Might get a large letter S out of this.*

I like to think that on that day, when Marvin Goldberg called me over to the white bulletin board, I took my first serious steps toward becoming a man. In fact, I believe that the tracks were being laid toward my adult understanding of life and, in particular, the Christian life. Goldberg was inviting me to discover *resilience*, a very important term in my spiritual journey. Now I know that I learned about resilience first as an athlete and then, later on, ever so slowly, as a follower of Jesus.

That's why the story of Marvin Goldberg threads its way through this book. What he taught me at the age of sixteen is largely the way I choose to live at the age of sixty-five.

That infamous day, the coach was not asking for an immediate answer. Instead he said, "I want you to leave the track and think about what I've said. And when you decide what you want to do, come back and let me know."

A day later I told Marvin Goldberg that I would trust him and that I would be willing to pay the price. The day after that, my name appeared for the first time on the third sheet of the seven pages stapled to the white bulletin board.

Eight months later, I wore my first white cardigan sweater with a large *S*.

———

ALMOST FIFTY YEARS LATER

A few years ago, the headmaster of the Stony Brook School invited me to give the baccalaureate address at the school's upcoming commencement festivities. I responded with an immediate and grateful yes. Even though the event was several months away, I began to visualize what it would be like to return to that beautiful campus that was home to me for three years during the 1950s.

I loved Stony Brook and have always appreciated the sacrifice my parents made to send me there. The men and women who were my instructors and mentors had been solid, mature, noble people. In them I had gained a wonderful composite picture of healthy manhood and womanhood. I saw examples of good marriages, exceptional character, and agile minds. And, for me, no one had epitomized all of this more than Marvin Goldberg.

Now, decades later, I was to return as the baccalaureate speaker. I wanted my wife, Gail, to go with me. Furthermore, I wanted our two oldest grandchildren, Erin and Lucas, to share the experience. I could see myself squiring them around the campus, pointing out the places where special memories had once been forged.

I would first take them to the library, I thought, where I had spent innumerable hours with books. Then I'd want them to see my old dorm room on the third floor of Hegeman Hall where I'd enjoyed a memorable senior year.

I intended to also visit the chapel, a beautiful traditional house of worship with a small steeple. I'd often retreated to its small sanctuary after track practice and played the piano as dark descended over the campus.

But the best moment in the visit to Stony Brook would be when I took Gail, Erin, and Lucas with me to the track where I had spent so many afternoons. I imagined showing them the white bulletin board and describing my moments of anxiety as I sought my name on that third sheet and learned what workout Coach Goldberg had in mind for me.

Finally, the weekend of our visit came. And, just as I'd planned, we visited the library, saw my old dorm room, and peeked into the chapel. Then it was off to the track.

But the track—my track—was not there. Everything, in fact, was different. The track had been relocated, and the new one was nothing like the one I'd known. This one had a state-of-the-art, all-weather running surface. I think I could have set world records on this new track!

The white bulletin board? Also gone! What had happened to it? And why was I so disappointed not to find it?

My deep sense of nostalgia was testimony of how much of my life was changed during those Stony Brook years. I went there a boy; I graduated a young man. I went there wondering what was expected of me in life; I graduated with some answers. I went there seeking models of Christian maturity; I graduated having found them. And a large part of these discoveries happened on Marvin Goldberg's running track. Maybe that's why I was so shaken when I discovered it was gone.

For three years, almost every afternoon, I had gone to the white bulletin board, spiked running shoes in my hands, to study the day's workout plan. None of the workouts was ever easy, and, until I finally learned that the coach would never back down, I sometimes tried to amend some of my workouts.

"Sir, did you really mean that I should run ten 400s today? I don't know if I . . ." "Sir, I'm wondering if there's any chance your pen slipped when it wrote five miles for a stamina workout." It was easier to blame Goldberg's pen than Goldberg himself.

"Sir, we did twelve step-down 200s yesterday; did you really intend that I was to do fifteen today?"

"Sir, I have a cold. I have a splitting headache. I've got shin splints . . . Sir, I think I'm dying."

"Now, Gordie," he would say to me, "why don't you start your warm-ups? You'll feel much better when you've loosened up." MWG wasn't a negotiator. He had plans for his runners, and he intended to stick with them. He knew what I (and others) was capable of accomplishing, which is to say that he believed in us far more than we believed in ourselves.

But let me say it again for emphasis: what I didn't understand then (but do now) was that Goldberg was looking ahead to life when we were in our thirty-fifth, forty-seventh, or fifty-eighth year—when we might bear much greater responsibilities and would have to reject the seductive call of sniffles and headaches and other distractions so we could do what had to be done. At fifteen and sixteen he was helping us learn for the first time that the satisfactions of life go to the man or woman who pursues self-control and who is willing to push the body and mind beyond natural points of resistance. We were thinking of the hymn writer's "flowery beds of ease." He was thinking . . . *resilience.*

Today—forty-five years later—Coach Goldberg lives in heaven. But he also lives in the core of my being. Few days go by that I do not remember his impact on my life.

In my sixty-fifth year of life, I am running along Shaker Road in our little rural New Hampshire town. There is a bit of a drizzle; my legs feel heavy. And a voice from within proposes that I turn back.

And then the coach speaks from somewhere in my memory: "Quit now, Gordie, and you'll make it just a bit easier to quit something more important later on." So I keep going because the coach insists.

I am crowding a deadline for something I've promised to write. A part of me wants to e-mail the editor and tell him that I'm too busy and cannot fulfill my obligation. And Goldberg speaks up again: "Gordie, you have a commitment to fulfill; you gave your word."

A grandchild calls to ask if we can get together. Momentarily, I'm tempted to beg off because I have pressing matters that seem important. And I hear the coach say, "Gordie, men and women like myself were there for you. Think about it . . ."

In my busyness, I am tempted to blow off the need to take time to quiet my soul and listen to God. More often than not, in moments like these, the coach speaks up: "Gordie, how often have we discussed the importance of your workouts and how they prepare you for the race? Your stamina is everything, and it's built day by day as you give yourself to the workouts. Do your soul work in the same way."

I tell you, the coach "lives." And what do I keep hearing from him? That the race of life is a race of distance, not a sprint. I must cultivate a spiritual life that covers that entire distance and *never* loses sight of the race leader, Jesus. This is the start of the resilient life.

IN RETROSPECT

At Stony Brook I became a very good runner, but I never became the *great* runner that Marvin Goldberg envisioned me to be. While I did win most of the races I entered, and while I collected a varsity letter for every season I competed, the fact is that I could have done much, much better.

Perhaps it is a further commentary on Goldberg's view of athletic achievement that, in my senior year, when I was high point man on the team, he gave the Trackman of the Year trophy—the one we all coveted—to someone else, a runner who worked very hard and *exceeded* his goals. Me? In those days I was too often content to do just enough to beat my opponent. In the eyes of MWG, that was nice, but not enough to earn a trophy as trackman of the year.

But that doesn't mean I didn't absorb a very powerful lesson that has stuck with me for these fifty years. What I took away from those days on the track was an understanding of Marvin Goldberg's method for building athletes and, more importantly, a pattern by which to live the Christ-following life. I didn't appreciate then how deeply I would be marked by Coach's ways—that almost every day of my life from that point on, I would reach back and apply one of his principles in the way I made my choices and set my direction for each day.

If MWG's immediate goal was to develop resilient athletes, I think his longer-range goal was to build resilient Christian men. One day he said to his cross-country team, "When you near the finish line tomorrow, I want you to sprint, even if no one is near you, and I want you to continue running a good pace for another quarter mile *past the finish line.*" We were incredulous. Run five miles (plus), then sprint, and then keep going for an extra quarter?

"Sir, you're kidding. Aren't you?"

"Gordie, you can be sure that the teams next on our schedule will hear that Stony Brookers do this, and it will convince them that we are much better conditioned than they are. It will give them something to think about." That we were better conditioned was generally true, anyway.

Many years later I recalled this strategy of sprinting across the finish line and running the extra quarter mile, and I laughed. Goldberg wasn't really that worried about other teams. This strategy was really for us. It was meant to convince us that we had far more stamina than we believed we had. And furthermore, it was to teach us the importance of finishing any kind of race in life with vigor and to exceed the minimum requirements.

As the years have gone by and I have thought a thousand times about my days on Stony Brook's dirt running track, I have concluded that my basic formulation of the Christian life was forged there under Marvin Goldberg's coaching. Perhaps if he were with us today, he'd use other words, but I think he'd agree with me that he was trying to make four things happen.

First, he wanted his athletes to run with a big picture of great possibilities in their hearts and minds. He could not bear the thought of an athlete who would leave unfulfilled potential on the track when the last day of the season arrived.

Second, he insisted that his athletes look backward and learn from yesterday's experiences. There was something to be learned from both victories and defeats.

Third, MWG taught his athletes to love self-discipline and to beware of the temptations of self-indulgence.

"I want to make your practice painful," he would say, "so that the race will be a pleasure." It was his way of reminding us that life is full of occasional hardships. We should get used to it.

Self-discipline was an issue in every part of life, in little things as well as big. One minute, self-discipline might mean pushing to break a personal record on the track. In another moment, it might be a matter of seemingly insignificant details.

As we were boarding the team bus one day for a trip to another school, the coach stopped me. "Gordie," he said, "your necktie is loose. Tighten it up, please. Stony Brookers travel with dignity."

Another time I was standing at the starting line of an 800-meter race. The runners were pawing at the ground with their spikes, waiting for the starter's pistol to be raised. Suddenly, I heard a quiet voice just behind me: "Gordie, the back of your shirt isn't tucked into your shorts. Stony Brookers wear their uniforms with pride."

The senior class had planned a party that would go late into the night. "Gordie, I'm sure you've looked forward to Friday night, but you have a race on Saturday afternoon that might make the difference in the team's chance to win, and I'm going to ask you to leave the party by 9:30."

Finally, MWG wanted his athletes to be proud to be part of a team, a "happy few" who were committed to making great things happen.

Marvin Goldberg believed in the power of a team. He foresaw the day when each of us would either be leaders of teams or members of one. Here in our teen years he was committed to teaching us how to contribute to each other's lives and how to receive from one another.

Often when a runner was at the starting line to compete in a crucial race, Goldberg made sure that the rest of the team was spotted at each turn and along the straightaways so that, during the race, our man would never be out of earshot of someone's encouragement.

In my study is a wooden baton that was carried four laps around a running track by a relay team that won the mile relay in a major prep school championship track meet. On the baton are all the names of my fellow trackmen. As I study those names from time to time (the ink faded), I have a memory and a mental photo of each of them. We were a band of brothers (as Shakespeare once put it), a "happy few," and Goldberg had welded us together into a team.

It's important to note that we, *the runners and the field men*, were the team. Goldberg was the *coach*. There's a difference. MWG never tried to be a friend or a peer to his trackmen in order to win their loyalty. Until we graduated, he was a coach: *Mr. Goldberg* or *Coach* or *Sir*. It was only when we graduated that he said, "Why don't you call me Marvin?"

If he was not a friend during our running days, who did the coach most resemble, in relational terms? Answer: he was a father. And that was what we needed in those days, a father, because we were absent from our real fathers, and we were just kids.

Many are the memories of the coach's hand on my shoulder and his quiet, calm voice offering a word of advice. Almost always he began, "Now, Gordie, . . ."

That is how Marvin Goldberg developed resilience in his boys. And, without ever knowing it, he gave me the footprint for this book. For the resilient life—getting stronger as I get older—is developed much the same way Marvin Goldberg built his athletes.

Thank you, sir, for teaching me this.

Resilient People Are Committed to Finishing Strong

They believe that quitting is not an option.

They know that "walking" is unthinkable.

They are convinced that building

resilience is a daily pursuit.

They despise aimlessness.

They have the faces of champions.

ONE

QUITTING IS NOT AN OPTION

When my mother died some years ago, I telephoned a very distant cousin (my mother's niece) to pass along the news. Our conversation lasted far longer than I'd anticipated, because she began to tell me stories about my mother's family that I had never heard.

My mother was the last of eight children born into a Swedish immigrant family. Now, with her death, all eight were gone. "Your mother's family was a bunch of quitters," my cousin said bluntly. "When life toughened, the brothers drank and the sisters complained. Then they simply gave up and died . . . one by one."

The remark haunted me long after the phone call ended. "*Quitters!*" she'd said. Not a particularly ennobling thing to say about a family line. Because I could not dismiss my cousin's judgment, I began to reassemble the pieces of my mother's life as best as I could recall them.

She had tried hard to be a good mother to my brother and me. But time and again, my mother had tasted disappointment. Lots of things simply didn't work out for her. She would get a job but give it up in a short period of time. She would start projects around our home but rarely finish them. She would announce that we were going to do family life in a new way, but the resolve to change would not last.

Mother seemed to be a busy person, but very little ever got done. She knew a lot of people, but I'm not sure there were many intimate friends. Only one comes to mind. She had talents (playing the piano was one of them), but I don't think any of them were ever developed.

There is in our home a small painting that my mother started in her older years. I prize it as one of the few keepsakes she left behind at her death. But the painting was actually finished by another person.

I loved my mother, and I am grateful to her for being faithful to her two sons. But I am also aware that orderly, disciplined, durable living for her was a continuous struggle. And while I know that her death was the result of a massive stroke, I fear that she died of a broken, unfulfilled heart.

Before the conversation with my cousin, I had never connected the dots of my mother's life in such a way that I could see these underlying patterns. A single pejorative word—like *quitter*—can sometimes make that happen. Now, spurred on by that word, a lot of things became clear to me—about my mother and *about myself*. Finishing things was a challenge for both of us. It marked our character.

The best way I could put it was this: *I had a quitter's gene in me.* Forgive me if this is not a clinical statement that a psychologist might recognize. But it explains things to me, even if it is a harsh self-assessment . . . of my mother, of myself.

Marvin Goldberg may have been the first, I think, to sense the hint of a quitter's gene in me when I was a high-school boy. During the summer before my last year of prep school, I decided that I wanted to quit his cross-country team. I was tired, I had concluded, of grueling workouts. I wanted some free time so that I could (how do you say this in a serious way?) do more dating and anything else that comes under the rubric of freelance fun. Athletic life was not compatible with such desires.

Come spring, I told myself, I'd get serious again and run on Goldberg's track team, but I wanted out of the fall schedule of long-distance competition, where our team frequently contended in 10k races against college freshmen teams.

Since vacation times were spent at home—two thousand miles away from the school's campus—I chose to say all of this in a letter. Frankly, I would never have had the audacity to say these things to the coach in a face-to-face conversation. He would have cut through my defenses in minutes. So a letter was the better way, I determined. And when I wrote, I tried to make my decision sound like serious reasoning, as if the determination to "party" rather than run was God's will or something.

Within a week there was a return letter. MWG had wasted no time with his reply. As I recall, his typed letter was several single-spaced pages long. I wish I still had it. Because even I, a young, immature teenage kid, could see that the man was thinking about a lot of things greater and longer lasting than just whether or not I continued as a runner that fall.

I remember that my father asked to see what Goldberg had written. When he finished reading it, he said, "This may be the most important letter you will ever receive." Perhaps his was a bit of an overstatement, but he certainly gained my attention.

In short Goldberg had said this: "By not running with the cross-country team this fall, you will have made the following choices: You will have disappointed your teammates, who depend upon you to help them win races. You will have turned your back on the team's supporters, who have shown up at every race in the past to cheer on athletes like yourself. But most of all"—and here he went straight at the jugular vein—"you will have inadvertently reinforced a danger-ous character trait: specifically that whenever you are faced with a challenge you don't like, or that seems too difficult, or that asks from you too great a sacrifice, you will find it easier and easier to walk away from it" . . . in other words, *to quit.*

Goldberg knew nothing of what I was to learn about my mother many years later. But I think he detected the quitter's gene.

His letter and my father's endorsement of it overcame my quitter's instinct, and I changed my mind, returned to the cross-country team, and helped lead it to a league championship that year. I cannot claim that I enjoyed myself in that effort, but at a deeper level I learned the satisfaction of accomplishing something that ended well. Perhaps satisfaction is more important than enjoyment in the long view of life.

Goldberg's letter had put a warning shot over the bow of my life. He was right. The temptation to give up in the face of difficult challenges has never been too far from my thinking over these many years. Over and over again—to this day—when I am tempted to procrastinate, to abandon a commitment, to desert an effort, I remind myself of the day I returned to the cross-country course as a teenager and did something I didn't want to do. And in a heart-level dialogue with the part of me that lacks finishing-power, I say, "I finished then; I'm going to finish now. I did it well then; I'm going to do it well now."

These two stories—of my mother's life and a teenage decision—are among a number I could recite that speak to the issue of resilience in my own life. It's something I've had to work at, and every ounce of effort has paid off.

Wherever I have gone and talked about the resilient life, I have insisted that one must anticipate that the greatest contributions God has for us to make will happen in the second half of life. You should see the reaction if I add, "And you folks under forty? In actuality, most of what you're doing now is simply running the first laps of the race."

Caleb of the Old Testament is, of course, the great champion of the second half. "Give me the hill country," he begged Joshua. "I am eighty-five, and I'm as strong as I was at forty-five." (See Joshua 14.) I get the feeling that he said this in front of a score of young men who were maneuvering for easy assignments when it came to occupying the promised land. The hill country was full of walled cities and men who were rumored to be giants. Who'd want to tackle that? The old guy did.

On occasions when I have talked about Caleb and his resilience, I have invited response from the audience. I ask, "What is the most provocative word or idea that you've heard in the last little while, the one issue you might even take home with you and choose to think about?"

Invariably, someone responds, "The thought that I could keep on growing and that I could be like Caleb and make my most valuable contributions in the second half of life." It's not unusual, after the meeting ends, for some to linger and to say, "Thanks for giving me hope that my best years are ahead." I have seen tears in the eyes of people who say this. Somehow they feel that the first forty years have been more or less a failure. They didn't do a great job raising their kids. They squandered a marriage. They followed second-class priorities. And now, at midlife, they contemplate forty years of regretting wasted opportunities.

This doesn't have to be. The Christian worships a God who can (and does) take the life of any person, turn it inside out, and use it to build a piece of His kingdom.

———

The story of Eli, the Old Testament priest, grabs me. Here is an old guy who miserably failed both as a father and as a spiritual leader to Israel. He should have been fired with cause. But something happened in his life that the Bible does not fully describe. All we know is that God used him to coach a young boy, Samuel. It was as if Eli said to himself one day, "I've blown everything else in my life; I'm not going to blow this opportunity."

Under Eli's mentoring, Samuel grew up to be one of the greatest prophets in all of Israel's history. You can read his story in 1 Samuel. For Eli it was a significant achievement in his second half of life. To be sure, he had to live and die with some of the consequences of his earlier failures, but he did give Israel a fiery young leader. There's at least *some* resilience here.

Among my favorite Bible stories is the one told of Paul and his apostolic teammate, Silas, who were beaten and thrown into a Roman prison because they were disrupting the peace by preaching the Christian gospel in the streets of Philippi. "About midnight," the writer says, "Paul and Silas were praying and singing hymns to God, *and the other prisoners were listening to them*" (Acts 16:25, emphasis mine).

I smell resilience. Here are men who have been manhandled by a mob—illegally, it turns out—beaten to a pulp, imprisoned under unspeakable conditions, and they are singing. And their songs are not only strength-giving to themselves, but other prisoners are apparently enriched by their behavior. One could say that a jail was transformed into a sanctuary by two resilient men.

A few weeks before my very-ill mother died, she and I had a long conversation about a broken relationship in her life. She wept freely as she recounted the many ways she felt she had contributed to the demise of the relationship. It was clear to me as she talked that her sense of failure in this matter was overwhelming, that, in some ways, it typified her own view of her whole life.

As best I can recall the conversation, a part of it went like this:

"Mother, why do you let your thoughts drag you down? Why don't you acknowledge your sense of responsibility and ask for forgiveness?"

"I'm not sure that [she named the other person] would ever talk to me again."

"You can write a letter, and perhaps that will get things started."

"I don't have the strength."

"Mother, tell me what you'd like to say. I'll write the letter, and then you can judge whether or not I've expressed your heart."

"I'll try."

My mother listed all the issues for which she felt responsibility in the broken relationship, and after she had exhausted herself in the recounting, I retreated to the other side of the room and wrote the letter while she napped.

When I was finished and she had awakened, I said, "I've written what I heard you saying. Let me read it to you so that you can tell me where I need to make changes." I began to read. Again, there were many tears as she heard words that expressed her thoughts.

"Underline that phrase," she might say as she listened. "No, I'd rather you said it this way." Little by little the letter grew in the strength of its repentant character. Finally, we were finished with the editing.

"I've wanted to say all that for ten years," she said. And I thought to myself, *My mother has carried an intolerable load of regret and sorrow all of these years. Why did she allow the burden to get so heavy?*

The letter was delivered the next day. Not long after, a response came from the one to whom she had written. It was an assurance of forgiveness. And it was instantly evident that my mother felt immensely lighter.

My mother had finished something important. A few weeks later she finished her race and went to be with Jesus.

TWO

"WALKING" IS UNTHINKABLE

———

For all the admiration we have for the earliest generations of the Christian movement, we must not forget that the quitter's gene was not unknown in those days. The people to whom the New Testament book known as the Letter to the Hebrews was written, for example, apparently struggled with the hideous pressures of maintaining faith in a non-Christian world.

Families were separated; people were banned from long-standing social connections; there was scattered physical persecution. The price for declaring that one had organized his or her life around Jesus was high, to say the least. The result? More than a few people went just so far, and then they quit, dropped out of the race.

This wave of quittings birthed serious questions among those who persevered. Did these quitters have faith and then lose it? they wondered. Or was theirs a bogus faith from the very beginning? The writer to the Hebrews wrestled with these questions.

In our Western society, where Christianity has more or less prevailed for centuries, it would be absurd to liken life to that which the first Christians faced. There are certainly occasional stories of pressures similar to those in ancient times. But the issue of quitting takes on a different look in our time. We are a people who are, in most cases, destined to live twice the length of first-century people (statistically speaking). Ours (at least in the immediate future) is not the question of buckling under overt and severe persecution; rather, we face the questions, *can one last and can one grow and can one actually contemplate being more valuable for the kingdom in the second half of life than in the first?* Resilience for first-generation Christians had a lot to do with real suffering. Resilience for us has, in most cases, more to do with *lasting* and *thriving* in the spiritual way.

Let me pause in my development of this thought to say that I am aware that some of my books have reached places such as China and North Korea and into parts of Russia. There they may be read by people who feel they have far more in common with first-century Christians in terms of suffering for the faith than most of us in the West. If such people compliment me by reading this book, I want them to know that everything I write about resilience pertains to such a world as theirs. I want them to know that I have them in mind.

In the eleventh chapter of Hebrews there is a crescendo of enthusiasm as the writer looks back across the history of biblical people and notes the championlike behavior of people who had faith, who didn't quit. Abel, Enoch, Noah, Abraham and Sarah, Joseph, and Moses are on the list. Gideon makes it; so do David, Samuel, and then a much larger roster of unnamed heroes who "conquered kingdoms, administered justice, . . . shut the mouths of lions, . . . were tortured . . . stoned . . . put to death . . . destitute," to name a few of the difficulties (vv. 33–37). "These were all commended for their faith," the writer concludes (v. 39). He describes people whose common characteristic is in fact a *resilient* faith. These are the great ones who didn't quit!

Having constructed this literary hall of fame, the writer then advanced to the twelfth chapter and wrote some of the most provocative biblical lines I have ever read:

> Therefore, since we are surrounded by such a great cloud of witnesses [the people in the preceding paragraphs], let us throw off everything that hinders and the sin that so easily entangles, and let us run with perseverance [read *resilience* here] the race marked out for us. Let us fix our eyes on Jesus, the author and perfecter of our faith, who for the joy set before him endured the cross, scorning its shame, and sat down at the right hand of the throne of God. Consider him who endured such opposition from sinful men, so that you will not grow weary and lose heart. (Heb. 12:1–3)

This writer had been to the games more than once. He had stood close to the starting line that the runners tensely approached as the starting judge barked out, "Runners, take your marks." It was the signal to strip off all clothing. (Runners in the ancient games took it *all* off—they ran naked.) "Everything that hinders," the writer said.

Today, modern athletes wear track outfits that have been engineered to minimize body friction. Clothing is almost like a second skin. Running shoes could not be lighter. In a race where first and second place may be separated by 1/100th of a second, it is the little things, like an unnecessary ounce of material, that matter.

"Run with resilience . . ." *Resilience* is the word that describes the toughened condition of both the body and the mind. In this description, my own sense is that the writer has a marathonlike race in mind, one that takes runners across the countryside on a course of roads and paths "marked before us." Those of us who have run such a course know that the markers may be orange cones, flags on posts, gates in a fence or wall, or temporary barriers or ropes erected to guide the runners toward the finish line. All along the way are race officials calling to the runners and pointing the way around turns. Sometimes they yell out the accumulated time for each mile run. And they often have bottles of water to hand out to dehydrated runners.

I suspect that the writer is imagining a race of teams such as the cross-country team I ran with in prep school and in college. The best seven runners from each school go to the starting line. Usually they are arranged in single file behind the lead runner. When the gun sounds, the teams take off down the course, and soon all of the runners are bunched together in a fusion of school colors. The lead runners are usually out in front setting the pace.

Our cross-country team ran what was called a one-three-three model. The "one" was our lead runner (I'll call him John), and the two "threes" were runners clustered together by the coach because of their comparative running skills and their compatibility with one another. Both "threes" took their cues in terms of pace from John, the "one."

In our own team cluster, we urged each other on and maintained, together, a racing strategy set forth by Marvin Goldberg. He had walked the course with us and pointed out the places where we should accelerate past runners ahead of us.

This New Testament writer seems to understand this way of racing. He poses Jesus as the "one," the lead runner. "Looking unto Jesus" (KJV) he writes as he likens the Christian community to a team of runners.

John, our number "one," was a great runner. He was a mature athlete, quiet spirited, dependable, and hardworking. We, the other six, greatly respected him. And whenever I read the words of Hebrews 12 and get to the "looking unto Jesus" part, I think of John.

The number "one" in the race depicted in Hebrews is described as the author and perfecter of our faith. Christian faith starts with

Him, and it is magnificently modeled by Him, particularly in terms of resilience, which is where the writer is going with his message. The number "one" in our faith, Jesus, was not intimidated by either the physical suffering of the cross nor the psychological shock brought on by its humiliation.

Crosses, almost everyone knows, were reserved for the worst of criminals, and a crucifixion was an unspeakable way for any human being to die. It confounds the mind that the Son of God would be subjected to the most degrading treatment people of that generation could have conjured up. Yet He endured it . . . and He did not quit. This message—that faith's "number one" did not quit—is the burden of the writer of Hebrews.

Each fall, during my prep-school cross-country days, our team would compete at least twice at the legendary Van Courtland Park cross-country course in the Bronx of New York City. Today, some fifty years later, you can go to Van Courtland Park on any Saturday in the fall and see hundreds, sometimes thousands, of runners competing in race after race at the college and high-school levels.

Unfortunately, Van Courtland Park was bad news for John, our number "one" runner. For reasons I never understood, John developed a psychological block at a certain point on the Van Courtland Park course. When he reached that particular place, something in his will would break down and he would slow down and walk.

Stopping and walking, during a race or a practice, was the worst of all athletic sins in the mind of Marvin Goldberg. One simply didn't do this. Slow down if you must, but never(!) stop. And walking? Don't even think about it!

I remember the first time this happened. As the race opened up, John had moved ahead with a block of lead runners. Our group of three may have been thirty or forty meters behind. We were halfway, perhaps two-thirds of the way, through the race and came around a corner in the course. *And there was our "number one," John . . . walking!*

Shocked is a word we reserve for moments of total surprise. A moment when we simply don't know what to do. And *shocked* describes our group of three. *John was walking!*

Immediately, one of our group of three (not me) slowed down and started walking near John. Now we were a group of two. I could feel the other guy slowing his pace, and I wasn't doing so well myself. The team never recovered in that race. All of that comes to mind when I read, "looking to Jesus . . ." And I am reminded that *He didn't stop.* He powered His way through the crisis of the cross, through death, and experienced this grand resurrection, which Christians celebrate every year.

He "sat down at the right hand of the throne of God," the writer says. It's the seat of the winner, the most honored place. Many of us have been at such a place, where trophies and medals are given to the athletes who have finished first, second, and third. It is hard to think of more exciting moments in life than when one is awarded the prize for not only finishing, but winning. And Jesus was there.

Then the writer brings the meaning of his metaphor home: "Consider him who endured . . . that *you will not grow weary and lose heart*" (emphasis mine).

Among the heroes of modern faith from which I have taken much courage is E. Stanley Jones, the Methodist missionary and evangelist who spent more than fifty years of his life in India. At the age of eighty-three, after a lifetime of constant world travel during which he spoke to millions of people, met with presidents and prime ministers, and was instrumental in the conversions of countless people, he suffered a debilitating stroke. It left him without speech or physical mobility.

In his waning months before he died, Jones managed to mutter through virtually paralyzed lips the manuscript of a remarkable book. Short, admittedly disjointed at places, the book is E. Stanley Jones's final declaration of faithfulness to Jesus. In one amazing paragraph he writes:

There are scars on my faith, but underneath those scars there are no doubts. [Christ] has me with the consent of all my being and with the cooperation of all my life. The song I sing is a lit song. Not the temporary exuberance of youth that often fades when middle and old age sets in with their disillusionment and cynicism . . . No, I'm 83, and I'm more excited today about being a Christian than I was at 18 when I first put my feet upon the way.[1]

That's what resilience sounds like at the end of the race. And it's what the writer of the Hebrews letter was trying to get across.

THREE

BUILDING RESILIENCE IS A DAILY PURSUIT

———

Some of the world's best devotional literature was penned by early-twentieth-century author Oswald Chambers. But it wasn't until after his death in 1917 that his wife, Biddy, published much of his work, including his greatly acclaimed *My Utmost for his Highest*.

Chambers kept a journal, and in it we gain insight into his own spiritual journey. An entry in that journal reads:

> A great fear has been at work in my mind and God has used it to arouse me to prayer. I came across a man whom I knew years ago, a mighty man of God, and now ten years have gone and I meet him again—garrulous and unenlivened. How many men seem to become like that after forty years of age! The fear of sloth and indulgence has come home with a huge fear and fairly driven me to God to keep me from ever forgetting what I owe him.[1]

Two key words, both rather Victorian, mark this description of a person: *garrulous*, a word which suggests someone who talks a lot but says little; and *unenlivened*, a person whose spirit seems deadened. It is not a complimentary portrait.

In his letters to Timothy, Paul reflects a concern for the younger man that is not unlike Chambers's fear for himself. Timothy had gone to Ephesus, where he had apparently assumed pastoral responsibilities for the community of Christians in that area. He seems to have been a person of deep care and compassion. Paul had once written of him, "I have no one else like him, who takes a genuine interest in [people's] welfare . . . Timothy has proved himself" (Phil. 2:20, 22).

But if Paul was bullish about Timothy as a caregiver, he was less confident of Timothy's resilience. A reading of Paul's two letters to Timothy suggest that the younger man was too easily intimidated by powerful, older people, that he might have been reluctant to call people to a hardier level of faith. And it's possible that Timothy was a tad less self-disciplined than he ought to have been. Thus Paul wrote to him:

> Don't let anyone look down on you because you are young, but set an example for the believers in speech, in life, in love, in faith and in purity. Until I come, devote yourself to the public reading of Scripture, to preaching and to teaching. Do not neglect your gift, which was given you through a prophetic message . . .

> Be diligent in these matters; give yourself wholly to them, so that everyone may see your progress. Watch your life and doctrine closely. Persevere in them, because if you do, you will save both yourself and your hearers. (1 Tim. 4:12–16)

Paul is challenging Timothy to scour his life, to place it—as it were—under a microscope and assure that every part of it is operating according to the highest of Christian standards.

"Set an example" for people, he urges Timothy. In other words live in such a way that people want to follow you. The literal rendering of Paul's words are, "Stamp yourself on people's lives."

Paul's notion of Timothy's influence is broad sweeping: in speech (the things you say and the way you say them), in life (the qualities of your living routines), in love (the characteristics of your personal relationships), in faith (the way you love God), and in purity (your moral life). In all of these ways, Timothy's life is to be a canvas upon which the Christlike life is painted and which people can study.

Henri Matisse once said, "Artists should have their tongues cut out." What could he have meant? Perhaps he was saying that the artist's message comes through paint on canvas, not through the chatter of words. I can hear Paul saying to Timothy, "If necessary, cut out your tongue and make your ministry effective by the sheer demonstration of the dynamism of your way of life."

"Watch your life and doctrine closely," he adds. Here Paul is advocating the importance of self-examination. It is likely that no one else will do this for Timothy, he reasons; he'll have to do it himself.

In his book on Dr. Paul Brand, the physician who did so much to advance the treatment of leprosy, Philip Yancey relates that Brand would regularly take baths in scalding water. His purpose was to discover if there were any parts of his body where he might have lost feeling, which would be a sign that leprosy had attacked him. This sounds similar to what Paul was asking of Timothy. It's not a call to morbid introspection about which many are cautious. But it is much more in line with the prayer of the psalmist, who cried out:

Search me, O God, and know my heart; test me and know my anxious thoughts. See if there is any offensive way in me, and lead me in the way everlasting. [I am tempted to change the last phrase to, "lead me in the resilient way."] (Ps. 139:23–24)

The search for resilience is a futile one if a person is unwilling to engage in a regular assessment of self along the lines of Paul's challenge to Timothy: *in speech, in life, in love, in faith, and in purity.* And that of course is merely a sample. The list could have been a bit longer.

I was in Europe one time conducting a daylong seminar called "Ordering Your Private World." In the room were about one hundred pastors and Christian workers. When I invited dialogue, a woman spoke out and said something that sounded like this: "If you were to come to my home, you'd find every book, every gadget, and every system known to man designed to help me order my private world. But none of them seem to work for me. I want to make the days and hours of my life count. But it seems as if, after I make all my lists and identify all the things I want to do, I completely lose my willpower. I've tried new starts too many times. And now I'm afraid to start again."

The obvious: there was a personal crisis reflected in those words. And when she said them, my mind leaped back to a time almost thirty-five years ago when I might have said something similar about myself.

I was in my early thirties when, in a moment of profound personal insight, I realized that the wheels of my life were beginning to spin with less and less traction. What this woman said that day in a moment of extreme vulnerability was on the extreme side of my experience, but I was able to identify with her. If I had not acquired an inner control of my life, it most likely would have spiraled down into steady-state mediocrity in every part of me. The quitter's gene was coming alive.

The truth is that, on many occasions, I had heard the lectures and read the books about building life with a longer vision in mind. But, like many young people, I didn't get it. I was too blessed with seeming boundless energy, with a self-confidence bordering on hubris, and a practical conviction that thinking quickly on your feet can get you just about anywhere. "Today" was the important hour; tomorrow could take care of itself.

What I was blind to was the fact that every "yesterday" was informing the "todays" of my life and that every "today" was formulating consequences that would become influential for the "tomorrows." They—the yesterdays, todays, and tomorrows—were all networked and interfacing with one another. They could not become compartmentalized.

Later, a few years into a life of attempted Christian leadership as a pastor, I was just beginning to figure this out. Not so clearly that the insights saved me from all catastrophic mistakes of the future. Anyone who knows me or knows of me is aware that I am well aware of what the bottom looks like. But in my early thirties, I suddenly knew that I had to make some massive alterations in my personal conduct of priorities and convictions and take Paul's challenge to Timothy seriously.

Looking back with the insights of the accumulated years, I am certain that if I had not made some dramatic adjustments in the way I was living, nothing I enjoy today would be mine.

I'm not sure that I could have articulated the ground rules for the search for resilience the way I understand them today, but I must have intuited them nevertheless. Some of the basic ideas were these:

First, simply talking about the issue of resilience doesn't get one very far. Nor is there much value in talking about how badly everyone else needs it. Resilience belongs to the person who pursues it relentlessly for him- or herself.

Said another way, it's much easier to preach to others about resilience than to make sure one is (using Paul's words) "watching [his own] life and doctrine closely."

In both my writings and in my talks, I rarely miss an opportunity to quote a character in one of Scott Turrow's novels, who describes friends he's known for a lifetime:

Many years ago I learned their dirtiest, most crabbed secret.
That their passion to change the world derived from the fact
that they could not change themselves.[2]

Was Turrow reading my mail when he wrote those words? Did he know that, as a younger man, I was regularly talking about something I'd not mastered myself? How did he identify this human tendency of ours to preach hard and to lay a guilt trip on others as a kind of cover for our own sense of shallowness?

A second thing I learned about the pursuit of resilience was rather obvious but, nevertheless, important to acknowledge:

Developing resilience is demanding, mostly done in secret, often humbling, not always fun.

For me the foundation for understanding and applying this principle had been laid on the track and cross-country course. For five days of the week, we worked out, sometimes twice, maybe three times a day, and the experience could be a grueling one. With the exception of a few teammates who were wrestling with their own versions of the quitter's gene, there was no one to cheer anyone on. The workouts were often far more demanding than the race itself. In practice there were the tough corrections of a coach who wanted to see the best we could offer. Bodies were pushed to the limit, and if even one ounce of energy was left at the end of the day, it meant that I'd not given my best.

All of those memories of the tough workouts came rushing back to me years later when I recognized the parallels between the resilience I'd developed as an athlete and the resilience I had to develop as a spiritual athlete.

Saint Paul was talking that language when he wrote:

> Run in such a way as to get the prize. Everyone who competes . . . goes into strict training. They do it to get a crown that will not last; but we do it to get a crown that will last forever. Therefore I do not run like a man running aimlessly; I do not fight like a man beating the air. No, I beat my body and make it my slave so that after I have preached to others, I myself will not be disqualified for the prize. (1 Cor. 9:24–27)

Demanding? You bet. Developing spiritual resilience meant being harder on myself than most of us wanted to be. It meant regular self-examination in which speech and relationships and life choices are evaluated and, if necessary, corrected.

Done in secret? Absolutely. People who are developing resilience learn over a period of time not to talk too much about what they're into. Telling everyone what one is doing in the private moments of spiritual workout dissipates the quality and effectiveness of the experience. Matisse again: it's a time to cut the tongue out. Talk is cheap. "Just do it!" goes the well-known slogan.

Humbling? No question about it. When one exerts himself and steps forward to test God's promises, to seek His power, there are defeats, failures, occasional humiliations. Where others will simply walk away in denial or excuse making, the spiritual athlete stops and takes the heat. Why? To find out how to grow and acquire a deeper level of resilience.

Not always fun? The search for resilience is a *satisfying* experience; it is not always a fun experience. And satisfaction trumps fun!

I know how to have fun. You want to see fun? Follow my wife,

Gail, and me around for a while. We've learned fun. But fun alone does not build resilience. Toughness of spirit does.

A third principle in the search for resilience.

The pursuit of resilience never ends. It is a lifelong, calculated adventure.

I am not recommending this specific lifestyle as a prescription for any of us, but I am fascinated by the biblical description of Anna, one of two old people who recognized the Christ child when His parents, Joseph and Mary, brought Him to the temple for the first time.

There was . . . a prophetess, Anna . . . She was very old; she had lived with her husband seven years after her marriage, and then was a widow until she was eighty-four. *She never left the temple but worshiped night and day, fasting and praying.* (Luke 2:36–37, emphasis mine)

This description is an inspiration to me simply because it describes a person who never stopped pursuing personal growth and a desire to know God and His purposes. She dedicated her entire life to these things. Where she lived, apart from the temple, how she generated any income, whether or not she had any family is not in the picture. The writer simply wants to portray a woman who never stopped searching.

I am disappointed in the number of so-called Christian people whom I have met who opted out of the search for resilience at an early age. They stopped thinking and hinged themselves to ideas that are dangerously out of date. They maintain the semblance of a spiritual life that was developed in the past and which has never evolved and deepened to match the new realities of life. They slowly empty their spiritual tank of yesterday's zeal and vision and now merely go through the motions of a fantasy faith that makes no sense in the streets of the real world.

I am in my midsixties as I write this book. The challenge to deepen and enlarge my resilience is more real to me today than at any time in my life. I mustn't let a day go by without watching my "life and doctrine" closely, without adding to their muscle, without testing them to assure that they are genuine.

A fourth principle:

The search for resilience is dampened if one coasts on his or her natural abilities and talents.

Did I ever learn this one the hard way! Growing up in a pastor's home, I was blessed with certain understandings of leadership, a skill with words, a bit of charm in interpersonal relationships, and an ability to think quickly on my feet. The exact set of abilities one needs to run a church . . . for a while.

In my late twenties I put those skills to work when I first became a pastor, and they paid off for me. But I fear that what some people mistook for spiritual depth and wisdom was really a relatively superficial Gordon with a marvelous gift of gab. Perhaps I am being too hard on myself in order to make the point. But I'm safer on this side of the truth.

The fact is, I could not have lasted long at any level of Christian leadership, and I would have gradually dwindled down in my effectiveness as a spiritual leader if God had not pounced on my life and shown me my close-to-empty soul. I have written often of the moment when it became clear to me that I could no longer live in ignorance of exactly what Paul was telling Timothy to do. "Watch your life and doctrine closely." The truth was that I wasn't!

Thus the attempted switch: from living off of natural ability and adopting a life of intentionality in which—as I shall later describe in greater detail—I became more calculated and focused on goals and objectives, just as an athlete would reach for higher levels of achievement. That's what Paul was saying when he challenged Timothy to "be diligent about these things."

A final principle about the search for resilience.

The pursuit of resilience is difficult to measure on a moment-by-moment basis. It is a long-term investment in life.

Martin Buber wrote:

If you stand in front of a tree and watch it incessantly to see how it grows and to see how much it has grown, you will see nothing at all. But tend to it at all times, prune the runners, and keep the vermin from it, and—all in good time—it will come into its growth. It is the same with man: all that is necessary is for him to overcome his obstacles, and he will thrive and grow. But it is not right to examine him every hour to see how much has been added to his growth.[3]

We are talking about a lifetime here. We are focusing on the discipleship of a person who just may never be fully seen until the second half of life when wisdom, intellectual vitality, physical stamina, and deep spirituality finally come together and produce a person capable of doing great work for the advancement of Jesus' kingdom. Count on it: the second half of life can (and maybe should) be the best and most productive half of life.

There is no greater search than the one for resilience—that quality of spirit that increases the effectiveness of life with every passing year, that luminosity that elevates others to higher aspirations, that marvelous persona that reflects the Christ who ran the race as the "one" and who sits in the seat of victory now.

FOUR

THE FACE OF AIMLESSNESS

If resilience had a face, what would it look like? Recent conversations with two men (one young, the other quite old) come to mind. The one models resilience and the other something else. I'd call it aimlessness.

The younger of the two men had asked me if we might talk. He approached me at the end of a weekend conference for men, where I had been the speaker. My subject: *resilience*.

My talks had been wrapped around what I called "the critical question." I asked the men at the conference: "Do you have the spiritual stamina to run the entire race of life and cross the finish line with the kind of 'kick' [a burst of speed] for which so many great runners are known?"

The question apparently provoked this man who wanted to get together, and he concluded that he needed some help. We met for breakfast the next morning. Once we were served I said, "Tell me where you think you are in your life-journey."

His answer came after two or three minutes of silence while he doctored his coffee. Looking up, he said, "Your talks this weekend? They hit me hard. I feel as if I'm going nowhere."

"OK," I responded, struck by his bluntness. "What's inside those words?"

He thought for a minute and then started "streaming" his thoughts. "Well, my marriage sucks to begin with. I know my wife doesn't respect me. We've been married for twelve years now, and the only thing keeping us together is the kids."

"That it?"

"I hate my job. I have no idea if I'll even have work in the next few months, and I don't know what else I can do."

"That it?"

"My wife and I became Christians when Billy Graham came here about fifteen years ago. And she's taken it pretty seriously. She's in a Bible study and teaches kids in Sunday school. But . . . I don't know . . . I just kind of do church . . . come to things like these men's things. I guess I'm not into Bible study or anything. She wishes we'd pray together . . . but, you know, it's just not me."

"You're pretty hard on yourself," I said.

"But I deserve it, I guess," he said back. "Really, you know I'm just surviving from day to day. I've become a dull person going through motions. Know what I mean? I see my wife excited about the things she's doing. I see some of the guys I grew up with going places. And then there's me. I'm just plodding along, trying to keep my head above water, and my life seems to be going in circles. Maybe it's going someplace, but don't ask me where. See what I'm saying?"

That's my clearest recollection of our opening exchange.

"Any chance you're depressed?" I asked.

"Nah, I went to the doctor, and he said there's nothing wrong with me. I've just never had much willpower. Know what I'm saying?"

I asked lots and lots of probing, nosy questions. I suggested various ways of making a new start. I talked about the extreme makeovers (from the inside out) that happen when a person gets dead serious about following Jesus. But each question and each suggestion was parried by disappointing comebacks. "I've thought of that." "You know, I tried, but . . ." "That's not me." "Wouldn't work for me." "Don't want to."

"When was the last time you ever took a look at your life and determined that you would change something about it?" I wanted to hear about just one area of his personal life where he took a step forward.

"Oh, I think about things I'd like to change all the time. But I never end up doing anything about it. I'm just lazy I guess."

"So, who are your friends?" It's the last question I could think of.

"Hmm . . ." His answer took some thought. "Well, I . . ." He paused. And then he named a couple of men. "But they're really friends because they're husbands of my wife's friends. And if the women want to get together, the guys hang out a bit. I guess they're about the best friends I've got."

I begin to realize that my breakfast companion was seeking some "silver bullet" that would make all the indecision and inaction go away. He wanted someone to provide him with motivation and energy and capability, and do it cheaply, quickly, and painlessly. What he didn't want was for someone like me to tell him that he has a heap of personal work to do, and some of it was going to be difficult.

I had run out of things to say to him. It occurred to me that I had begun to take on the responsibility of finding a way to get this man's life in order and convincing him to do what I thought was best. That's a no-no in the world of counseling and is probably one of the reasons why I'm not that good a counselor.

But I am frustrated when I see a man wasting his life and unwilling to do anything about it. And I saw the possibility of myself in this man. *I could have become the kind of person this man describes himself to be,* I thought. *He's me . . . if there had not been men and women whom God sent into my life, like Marvin Goldberg, to push me hard until I got jump-started in a reasonably right direction.* Maybe that's why I kept pushing at this man. Because others did it for me. But in this case, nothing was working.

Finally I said what I was thinking and surprised myself with my candor. "You know, I want to say this respectfully . . . man to man. I've run out of things to say. I have no more questions; I don't have any more answers. You've obviously considered every idea I could suggest, and you don't see any of them as useful ways to address your dilemma. All I can tell you is that if you keep on this track, the second half of life isn't going to be much fun."

"Yeah," he said. "You're probably right." Strangely enough, he was not offended at me for being so confrontational.

"Why don't we arm wrestle for the check and be on our way," I said. "Let me think about what we've said to each other; perhaps I can recommend some other, smarter people for you to visit with, but I've told you everything I know. And I fear that the solution to the issues in your world really begins with you and what you think Jesus is asking of you, not with someone else's solutions."

He thought about that for a moment and then said, "OK. Well, I really appreciate the fact that you listened, and I'll let you know if I want you to look up any of those other people you mentioned. Thanks for getting together with me."

I never had a personal conversation with him again. We occasionally wave or share a smile across a room at a meeting, but he never renews the conversation with me. I do suspect he continues to have similar conversations with others who speak at conferences he attends.

In my journal is this comment from somewhere:

One of the saddest experiences is to awaken at old age and discover that one has been using only a small part of self.

Barring a magnificent life transition, my breakfast companion is on his way to such an awakening.

———

But I said there were two men and two conversations. If the account of the first of those two has left me feeling sad and empty, the second one fills me with hope.

FIVE

THE FACE OF A CHAMPION

I f there was a hall of fame for resilient people, I know a man who should be in it. Today he is ninety years old. He says we met when I was five years old, which means he's been a beloved friend for sixty years.

His name: Vernon Grounds, retired president of Denver Seminary, a man who has been a father-figure to me throughout my adult years. Sometimes I call him my father-in-faith.

The life of God is in this man, I say to myself when I sit down with him. There is a gentleness of spirit about him, and you feel it when you enter his presence and he moves toward you to give an affectionate hug.

Vernon Grounds can usually be found in his office in the middle of Denver Seminary's learning center on almost any school day. I much prefer, however, to think of his office as a chapel, which is where holy men like this one should spend their days. You do administrative things in an office. But you change lives in a chapel. And that's the business this man is in.

When Vernon Grounds retired from the presidency of the school in the mid-1970s, the succeeding leadership was wise to see the value of locating him at the center of student life. There he would become (my words) the soul of the school, available to any student, professor, or administrator (including the new president) who wanted to talk.

There were others in the school's hierarchy with whom one could discuss financial aid, course changes, and theological issues. But when one's life was in turmoil, when there were personal doubts about faith, and when questions of life-direction were at stake, Vernon Grounds was the go-to guy.

From my vantage point, Vernon is resilience personified. Long before I was old enough to conclude that Christian resilience was one of the biggest issues of life, I saw qualities in this man that I intuited to be the essence of Christian nobility. I made a conscious decision in my early twenties to become as much like him as I possibly could. Among the kindest compliments I have ever received is from the person who says, "When you said that [or did that], I saw Vernon in you."

So here I am, in this "chapel" of his. The walls are plastered with the pictures of men and women and their families who have passed this way in years gone by. That my picture is included in this mass of faces is very important to me.

Books everywhere. Stacks and stacks of books, obviously in the process of being read. The bandwidth of the man's literary interests is staggering. Sitting in his book-strewn office, I think back to our orientation days at seminary more than forty years ago when the then-president, eyes twinkling, had said to the entering class, "Buy books until you have to mortgage your marital bed. And then keep on buying." Many of us believed him (and obeyed) then . . . and still do. He caused us to love books.

What I came to appreciate over the years was that Dr. Grounds *actually got better and better as a person as the years went by.* And here he is now, at ninety, still a most sought-after man, still the kind of gentleman from whom all kinds of other people draw inspiration and resolve. How silly, I think, to ever tell people—as has our culture—that sixty-five is a retirement age after which you spend your life playing in Florida or Arizona. Here is a man whose most useful years have come *after* sixty-five, and he's still working.

Our conversation begins. Instantly, he pounces on me with questions. Always the questions: a Grounds trademark. Questions about my family, my work, my plans for the future. He wants to know what I'm seeing and learning about as I travel from here to there. He wonders if I know anything about common acquaintances. Then he moves on to soul questions: Do I still love God? Am I holding on to time in my wild schedule for spiritual development? What am I reading? And what do I think of . . . ?

There was a time when I could spend an entire hour with Vernon Grounds and do nothing but talk about myself in response to his questions. He felt no need to give *his* opinions or talk about himself. He was always keenly and genuinely interested in his guest. Then, as I matured, I began to ask questions of him. He would answer one or two and then deftly sidestep my questions and turn the conversation back toward me. And there I would be again: talking about myself.

But now, as old friends, we've improved on the balance. I've learned to coax him to open his life to me, and our conversation moves along at a delightful pace: rejoicing in news of both of our families, trading ideas and thoughts that have come from recent readings, wondering aloud (as old men do) where this world is going.

I have known only a few people in my life for whom I would reserve the word *saint*. This man is one of them. How did he get to be that way? And my answers to that question form the backbone of this book.

Vernon Grounds is the quintessential resilient man, because he has always thought about his life and the lives of others around him with a big picture in mind. He has always known the center of his strength and his call. And he has wasted little time out on the edges of activity where he is less competent.

His personal account of his conversion to Jesus is a specific one, although not a spectacular one. He never doubted for a moment that at a particular point in his young life, he made a life-altering choice to organize all of life around Jesus. Those who know him well are aware that no biblical phrase has marked him more powerfully than Jesus' words to the disciple Simon Peter, who often seemed distracted and scattered: "What is that to you? You must follow me!" And Grounds assumed this advice for himself.

Somewhere in his earliest years it became plain to him that he was a builder of people more than anything else. People simply grew under his influence, even when he was unaware that he was exerting it. They found order in their lives when they talked to him. They felt constrained to emulate his peaceable demeanor. They discovered a likeness to Jesus in his extended kindness.

As a man with an earned doctorate in the field of psychology, he could have pursued the life of a scholar or graduate-school administrator. But even though he bore the burden of a seminary presidency for twenty-five–plus years, as I see it, he was first and foremost a people builder.

Because this was clearly his call and his gift, he gave himself to it without ever striving for other forms of professional greatness or influence that might have been his. He understood that life was lived out of call and conviction, and his call was to build people according to God's design for them.

Result? Thousands of men and women today are doing what they are doing because his work with them was strategic.

A second piece of the puzzle that explains Vernon Grounds's resilience has to do with the fact that he never allowed any of the common adversities in his life to cripple or shrivel his soul.

I know Vernon well enough to have heard stories of his childhood. Some of his experiences were tough ones, and they could have so torn at his soul that he might have developed an edge of habitual anger or resentment toward some significant people in his youth. But that never happened.

In his days as an organizational leader, there was a bevy of critics and naysayers who took every opportunity to slander him, to question his motives, to make his work as a seminary president as difficult as possible. But I never saw him fight back or defend himself. That doesn't seem to have occurred to him. Instead he chose to be a grace giver.

Third, Grounds developed resilience because he determined to manage the routines of his life with intentionality. That's one of my words for discipline or self-mastery. He worked hard, but his work habits were healthy and productive. He was careful to prioritize energies and assets. One never got the feeling that he was striving to find a place of international Christian power or notoriety. He was not hungry for bigness in terms of reputation or opulence in terms of material acquisition.

Intentionality meant maintaining a relatively simple lifestyle, faithfulness to his family, loyalty to his church and the organization he led. It meant regular physical exercise, spiritual discipline, and a careful containment of all those ego-driven impulses that tarnish too many leaders. When I asked him what he thought was the secret of his long-lived vitality, he said with a contrived air of gravity, "God, gym, and genes."

When a student, I met my father-in-faith on countless occasions at a local restaurant for breakfast. I think every student at the school met him there perhaps as frequently as I did. He would sit at the same table every morning as if he owned it. I always suspected that the waitpersons (as they are now known) competed to serve him because he made their work a pleasure. They addressed him by name and with great respect. And they knew exactly what he would want to eat.

Toward the end of the breakfast, he would snatch the check and keep it out of anyone else's reach. If one protested, his familiar rejoinder was, "Someday when you become a wealthy pastor [a joke in itself], you can pay the bill. Oh, and you can also give generously to the seminary."

Now, many years later, if we have lunch or breakfast together, I have learned to arrange with the waitperson to get the check before we place our order. When he frowns at this tactic, I remind him of the deal he made years ago. Given the number of checks he picked up in my younger days, I have a long way to go before the score is evened.

Intentionality for Vernon Grounds means intellectual rigor and spiritual depth. Long before we had a generation of evangelical Christians who saw the importance of intellectual depth, Grounds pursued a PhD in psychology. Spiritually, he sought the heart of God, and his preaching and teaching showed a remarkable depth of insight into Scripture and its application to faith. Anytime the word got out that Vernon was preaching, a crowd gathered.

Again and again the reader or listener is left breathless with the breadth of knowledge from which Grounds draws to express his love for the gospel or his challenge to people to grow in Christlikeness. It all smacks of an intentionality to grow and keep on growing until his last breath.

Finally, Grounds has always understood the importance of key personal relationships that are marked with loyalty and mutual care. The people who worked with him have always loved and respected him. They smile at his eccentricities and enjoy his unusual manner-isms. And they support him—I suspect would die for him—because they know he loves them and puts them first.

I have been the recipient of that great relational skill of his many times in my life. When I was a troubled teenager, he would invite me to breakfast for a talk. When I was breaking into public ministry, he was there to remind me that God knew my number and would call me when I was ready. When I had major decisions to make, he was prepared with questions and insights that brought me certainty. And when my life fell to pieces years ago, he was present to help me put the pieces back together again.

Today, Vernon Grounds and his wife, Ann, live on the tenth floor of a residence for senior people. The owners of the complex will do anything to keep the two of them happy, because they have figured out that their presence in that community of seniors is a key to everyone's sense of well-being. Go through the front door at 5:00 PM on most Sunday evenings, and you will see Vernon conducting a worship service while Ann plays old and familiar hymns on the piano. This man will never retire.

On this particular day, I have come to talk to my dear friend about his health and his strength. He's ninety, I remind him, but he's living as if he's twenty-five years younger. Amazingly, he allows me to ask the bulk of the questions. We sit close enough together that I can frequently put my hand on his arm just as he has so frequently done to me in the past. And I think, as we talk, *This is the kind of a conversation a father and a son are supposed to have, that two old friends are supposed to enjoy, that two people who love God and who dearly wish to live life with resilience are supposed to share.*

When the conversation is over and I must return to the airport, I find it hard to jerk myself away. His warm, fatherly embrace is a blessed experience, one that many men have longed for all their lives: the blessing of the father-in-faith. I fight tears all the way to the car.

This is what resilience looks like when it has a face. And it's a face that belongs in a hall of fame. A champion.

RESILIENT PEOPLE RUN INSPIRED BY A BIG-PICTURE VIEW OF LIFE

They have a sense of life-direction.

They foresee the great questions of life's passage.

They cultivate Christian character.

They listen for a call from God.

They are confident in their giftedness.

They live generous lives.

THE BIG PICTURE

"Gordie, come here, please." I had spent the afternoon on the track running through the workout plan that Marvin Goldberg had designed for that day. Now it was time to head for the showers, steal a few moments in the chapel at the piano, eat dinner, and head for an evening of study in my room at Hegeman Hall. But before I could leave the track, I heard those summoning words.

As usual, MWG was near the white bulletin board working on the statistics of each trackman's performance for that day. When I reached him, he said, "Dorothy and I would like you to come down to our home for dinner tomorrow evening."

The Stony Brook dining hall was a large, noisy place. Students sat around tables set for ten—eight students and a faculty member and spouse. The food was ample, but it was institutional, at best, and one learned to welcome any invitation that provided an escape. "Thank you, sir; I'd love to come."

The next evening I made my way to the tiny house the Goldbergs occupied and was welcomed at the door by Dorothy Goldberg, the coach's wife. As I anticipated, the dinner was a wonderful respite from the typical dining hall repast. Soon the dishes were being cleared away, and Mrs. Goldberg disappeared into the kitchen.

That was when Marvin Goldberg reached behind him to a bookshelf and drew a school notebook off a shelf. On the front cover I could see my name written in large black letters.

"I have something to show you," the coach said. He turned to the back page. I could see the writing at the top: June, 1957.

In another book—*Midcourse Correction*—I have written of this moment. There under the heading was a list of races the coach anticipated my running three years in the future. Next to each race were the times (minutes and seconds and *tenths of seconds*) which he expected me to run. They were his estimate of the *personal best* that I could reach before I left Stony Brook as a graduate.

I can still see that notebook with those projected times, all of which I was convinced I could never reach.

"Sir, those times are impossible."

But Goldberg reminded me that I had three years to get there. "Watch," he said as he turned the pages of the notebook from the back to the beginning. I began to catch on that he had designed a plan for every month of my prep-school running career. Each month called for continuous improvement. It was like a flight of steps, and if I would attain each step in the schedule, I would, one day—three years later—reach the levels he believed possible for me, levels that in my shortsightedness I thought *im*possible.

"Now, Gordie. The key to this plan is trust in your coach and your willingness to discipline yourself and work hard. I'm very confident that we can reach these goals if you're prepared to do that."

I was fifteen years old when Marvin Goldberg showed me that notebook. Until that time no one had ever talked to me about the architecture—the big picture—of my life. Fifteen-year-olds, like myself, tended to live in the moment. The only future plans we had in mind had to do with a date next Friday, Christmas vacation, a dreaded exam, and a letter (hopefully with money) from home.

But this was something different. This was a pathway or a staircase from now to then. A way of growing. You could say it was an example of the picture a mentor or a coach has for his protégé. Jesus had a similar picture for His disciples; Paul, a picture for Timothy; Aquilla and Priscilla, for the young preacher, Apollos.

This was my picture. A man had cared enough, believed in me enough, to sketch out a plan of almost forty months of athletic development.

Resilient people believe in such pictures—a big picture, I call it. As artwork goes, the picture may be impressionistic—somewhat blurry and open to consistent modification. But it is, nevertheless, a picture. And it provides direction, hope, and a framework for growth.

That night MWG set me on the road toward the pursuit of resilience. He handed me the first of many big pictures I would draw or have drawn for my life. Fifty years later I am still thinking about big pictures. The race is not over yet.

SIX

RESILIENT PEOPLE HAVE A SENSE OF LIFE-DIRECTION

Before I formed you in the womb I knew you,
before you were born I set you apart.
—THE WORD OF THE LORD TO JEREMIAH (JER. 1:5)

On a host of occasions I have read the familiar conversation between Lewis Carroll's Alice and the cat, which starts with her question, "Would you please tell me which way I ought to go from here?"

> The Cat: That depends a great deal on where you want to get to.
> Alice: I don't much care where—
> The Cat: Then it doesn't matter which way you go.
> Alice: —so long as I get somewhere.
> The Cat: Oh, you're sure to do that . . . if you only walk long enough.[1]

There is no pathway to resilience in this exchange. There is nothing special about the thought of a person who talks like this.

But listen to the difference here. Almost fifty years ago, Thomas Merton wrote:

> If you want to identify me, ask me not where I live, or what I like to eat, or how I comb my hair, but ask me what I think I am living for, in detail, and ask me what I think is keeping me from living fully the thing I want to live for. Between these two answers you can determine the identity of any person. The better answer he has, the more of a person he is.[2]

These are the words of someone who thinks with a big-picture view of life. He is dealing with the largest possible questions: *What am I living for? What keeps me from a full realization of what I'm living for?* In effect, Merton reduced everything down to two issues: direction and possible obstacles.

Merton reflects the thinking of one of the most resilient men who ever lived: Saint Paul.

> One thing I do: Forgetting what is behind and straining toward what is ahead, I press on toward the goal to win the prize for which God has called me heavenward in Christ Jesus. (Phil. 3:13–14)

This is where resilient people begin: with the biggest possible picture of things they hear God speaking into their lives. When there is no big picture (e.g., Alice's "I don't care . . ."), life comes to resemble a bunny track—a furtive darting to and fro, lots of motion, little direction. To borrow other words from Paul, we become people who are

> tossed back and forth by the waves, and blown here and there by every wind of teaching and by the cunning and craftiness of men in their deceitful scheming. (Eph. 4:14)

Stephen Ambrose's book *Nothing Like It in the World* tells the story of the building of the transcontinental railroad in America. "The railroad took brains, muscle, and sweat in quantities and scope never before put into a single project," Ambrose wrote in his eminently readable history lesson.[3]

Early in the story, Ambrose describes the moment when construction was to begin and certain California people decided that there ought to be a great ceremony. A host of dignitaries were invited to gather at the place where the first rail was to be laid.

One of those invited was Collis Huntington, perhaps the railroad's most important West Coast backer in California. But he declined, saying:

> If you want to jubiliate [celebrate] over driving the first spike, go ahead and do it. I don't. Those mountains over there look too ugly. We may fail, and if we do, I want to have as few people know it as we can . . . *Anybody can drive the first spike, but there are months of labor and unrest between the first and the last spike.*[4] (Emphasis mine)

Huntington was not romanced by *first* spikes, by premature celebration. It was the *last spike* in the process that grabbed his attention. Everything in between the first and last spike was his big picture, and until the picture was all filled in, he wasn't celebrating.

When construction of the railroad was finally completed in May of 1869, a last spike, a golden one at that, was pounded into place, and two locomotives (one from the east; the other from the west) moved forward until they touched. A telegram was sent to President Ulysses S. Grant: "Sir: we have the honor to report that the last rail is laid, *the last spike is driven*, the Pacific Railroad is finished."

"The last rail is laid, the last spike is driven" (emphasis mine). Now maybe Collis Huntington had something to celebrate.

When Saul of Tarsus first entered the pages of the Bible, he was a Pharisee: "a Hebrew of Hebrews," he describes himself (Phil. 3:5). That was the biggest picture of himself he could imagine. And it was the kind of orientation that led to his aggressive and cruel persecution of Christians.

But then his personal big picture changed on the road to Damascus. That was the point of his conversion—a whole new picture. Looking back on that day, he told King Agrippa that he'd seen Christ. "Who are you, Lord?" he'd asked.

> "I am Jesus, whom you are persecuting . . . Now get up and stand on your feet. I have appeared to you to appoint you as a servant and as a witness of what you have seen of me and what I will show you. I will rescue you from your own people and from the Gentiles. I am sending you to them to open their eyes and turn them from darkness to light, and from the power of Satan to God, so that they may receive forgiveness of sins and a place among those who are sanctified by faith in me." (Acts 26:15–18)

"I was not disobedient to the vision [read "picture"] from heaven," he told Agrippa (v. 19). And he never was. Despite facing virtually every form of human suffering and adversity that it is possible to experience, he forged straight ahead. The new vision made the difference, and his resilience grew.

This new orientation—you could call it a conversion—has been the mark of the great biblical people down through the ages.

Moses had a change of pictures. At forty he had a fuzzy notion of being kind to a few Hebrew slaves. In an impulsive moment, he killed an Egyptian and paid dearly for his shortsightedness. Within days he was fleeing Egypt to the desert, where he spent forty years getting a new, a much clearer, certainly a fresh vision of himself and how God might speak to him.

It took four decades to seek and gain a new picture, and when at the age of eighty (note this!) he heard God's voice in the burning bush, it said:

> "I am the God of your father . . . I am sending you to Pharaoh to bring my people . . . out of Egypt . . . I will help you speak and will teach you what to say." (Ex. 3:6, 10; 4:12)

Now Moses had his big picture and his marching orders. They never changed. Everything in his life, from this point forward, was measured against this large-view orientation.

Each of these biblical characters experienced a remarkable conversion of life. The eyes of their hearts were opened to a big picture, to what things would look like when the last spike was driven.

For some time I have contended that the contemporary concept of Christian conversion is far too small. It emphasizes the driving of the first spike—a choice to entrust life to Jesus—but tends to ignore the last one—what Jesus calls us to be and to do. And while there is room for gladness when everything begins, the real focus should be on the big picture—where this is all going, how one is growing, what it means to finish well.

In the lives of the disciples, it is clear that there was an invitation to follow, which the disciples accepted. But one sees relatively little attention paid to the beginning and far more attention placed on what the disciples were becoming. It was as if Jesus had a notebook for each disciple, which included a month-by-month plan of growth and preparation. The main events in their lives were not where the first spike was driven (or the first race run) but on the last spike.

The resilient life is one where a person lives every day in the pursuit of the big picture. The pieces of the picture? Perhaps these questions point us in the right direction.

Where am I headed, and what are the great questions that will challenge me along the way?

What kind of a person am I becoming as a result of this journey?

What does God expect of me as I run the race?
What have I been equipped to accomplish?

What can I give?

I can't live with Alice's perspective on the journey: "I don't much care where . . ." But I do aspire to Merton's: ask me what I'm living for, and ask me what gets in the way.

SEVEN

RESILIENT PEOPLE FORESEE THE GREAT QUESTIONS OF LIFE'S PASSAGE

Not long ago I gave some talks at a conference for worship leaders. These are the folks who lead the music and the exaltation portions of many church services. They were there to learn from each other and to hear from people who might have a word of spiritual refreshment for thcm.

When I first entered the meeting room, I was startled to realize that almost everyone present seemed to be a twenty- or thirty-something person. I think I am safe in saying that almost no one exceeded the age of thirty-five, except—and this smarts a bit!—me, the speaker.

Facing this bevy of youthful, hyperenergetic, and lovable people, most young enough to be my son or daughter, several unanticipated thoughts tumbled about in my head.

These men and women were charged (and presumably gifted) with designing and leading worship for their congregations. That meant they selected songs and Scriptures, said prayers, and, in general, attempted to escort people into the presence of God through acts of reverence. *They had better know their audience,* I thought: who the people were, how they felt, what their hopes and dreams were, and where they sensed or feared their lives were headed. They had better know something about the big pictures that others brought into the sanctuary.

When I was a young pastor in my early thirties, I remember thinking that almost no man over the age of forty-five ever visited with me about his personal life *unless* he had a problem that was so obvious that it could not be ignored. Rarely did anyone from the older generation open their hearts concerning their fears, their aspirations, their doubts or convictions, unless I poked and prodded with a bundle of questions.

Only after I'd grown considerably older did I figure out why there was this general silence. *They assumed I wouldn't, or couldn't, understand.* I wonder how many meaningless sermons I must have preached from my thirty-year-old heart into the heart of a seventy-year-old one.

And now, here I was, about to talk to worship leaders half my age. Now *I* was in the place of some of my former church members who were older. I was dealing with issues in my life, in my big picture, that almost none of the people in this room could comprehend. And yet they were charged with leading people like *me* into a worship experience.

How could they pray, design worship, familiarize me with God if they knew so little about what was happening in a life like mine? Instantly, I changed the introduction of my talk for that morning.

I began with these words.

"My wife, Gail, and I have been a part of a small group that meets together every month. Ours is not a Bible study group, nor do we follow an agenda dictated by someone's curriculum. We simply meet, eat together, and then tell the stories of our lives as they have unfolded during the month since we were last together. And then we talk about our anticipations of the coming month. We trade tales of our grandchildren, about visits to the doctor, about our experiences in serving in our various forms of Christian service. By the time we end, everyone knows the important aspects of everyone else's big picture. Then our evenings end with a time of fervent prayer.

"There is one subject that never fails to come to the table each month in our group—sometimes by way of a joke, a story, or a piece of information about someone. Know what that subject is?"

I waited for a moment to let people think, and the room grew uncommonly quiet as people tried to imagine what I had in mind.

Then I told them: "Death! The subject of dying always gets to the table. Know why?"

Now I really had their attention. I could almost sense their incredulity. When you are in your twenties and thirties, you rarely talk about death (at least not regularly, in a small group) unless it has been pressed into life through sudden tragedy. I went on.

"In our group we talk about death because we know that the odds are that one of us is going to die in the next few years. We are all in our sixties and seventies, and we are sure, without even having to say it, that death is a high probability for one of us in the near future.

"Every Sunday morning," I said, "each of you leads a substantial number of people into worship for whom death is one of the most important and frequently pondered subjects. How do the songs you pick, the style in which you sing them, the way you pray, and the comments you make speak into the uncertainties that some of your people have about death? Or are you only concerned for people in your own generation? Like yours, other generations are there seeking comfort, direction, challenge, certitude. Only for them, the questions are a bit different than they are for you."

I talked about the importance of big pictures, the ones that God paints for us and which are always in a state of formation. "Those pictures are largely defined by the questions that we are asking.

"The most important questions in *your* lives, for example, are those about career, willpower, and relationships," I continued. "There is little about those questions that interest me personally. Some of the more important questions for me at my age are about whether or not I'm needed any longer, about having the courage to live with pain and weakness, and if God is anywhere close to being pleased with the way I've lived a large part of my life. You have your life ahead of you; I have mine largely behind me.

"You're worship leaders," I went on. "How are you going to usher people into the presence of God if you don't know the questions that form the big pictures in the hearts of the various generations you are leading?

"I suspect that there are different questions for every age in life, perhaps every decade. Knowing them helps us to deal with people sensitively, and it gives us a better understanding of how to build a larger view of our own lives.

"Remember, you heard it here first," I concluded. "You won't be asking the same questions ten years from now that you are asking today."

When question-and-answer time came, some asked, "So what are the questions that correspond to each decade?" A few samples occurred to me, but I admitted that I had some homework to do. "I just know that there are questions for every age group, and that they are pretty consistent," I said.

And here's the kicker. *As the questions change, so does the content (and perhaps the form) of our spiritual interests.* "The questions," I said, "often become our way of approach when we go to the Scriptures looking for spiritual sustenance. They become a guide when we buy books. The questions form our approach to spiritual life. So if the way one does spiritual life was formed around twenty-something questions and one is now fifty, spiritual life will likely be obsolete and ineffective."

In each decade of life as the questions change, the Bible reader discerns new insights from the familiar Bible stories or teachings. The themes of prayer also change. The dangers and temptations inherent in the spiritual journey are modified. And in each decade of life, new decisions leading to deepening commitment present themselves. So, knowing the appropriate questions that we are likely to face at the end of the track in each decade of life just might help us become big-picture thinkers.

When I left the conference at the end of that day, I determined to identify as many of the significant questions that people are asking as they move through the decades of life. I became convinced that if I could do this, I'd know a lot more about big-picture thinking and resilience.

———

One evening, a while after my talk to the worship leaders, I was reminded of my pledge to identify the unique questions of each decade of life. Gail and I were hosting a group of forty senior people—men and women mostly over the age of seventy-five. For many years those who gathered that evening were once the leadership of the Concord, New Hampshire, congregation where I preach on many Sundays. Now, at this station in life, they live a bit more quietly.

During our time together, Gail invited the group to recall their memories of church life in former days. Suddenly the room lit up with as much energy as I'd seen in the room where the worship leaders had met.

We heard about choir pageants, missionary conferences, extended prayer meetings, building programs, and radio broadcasts, to name a few programmatic things. There were stories of faith, conversions, and vision. Then came the stories of testings, sadnesses, and disappointments. I could tell by the rapid-fire comments coming from all about the room that these seniors wanted to deliver a message: they owned big pictures of life too. *They'd accomplished great things . . . even if the younger generation in the congregation didn't know (or even care).*

As the moments passed, I was struck with how little we know about each other across the generations. And how important it is to understand what questions form the larger picture of another's life. This is the pathway to resilience: knowing what's up ahead, what we are likely to face, where the possibilities and the obstacles lie. These people had answers to the questions the worship leaders needed to ask.

So I began my pursuit of the great questions that fill in the blanks of so many big pictures.

———

When I engaged with twenty-somethings, for example, who were just entering the adult years, I found them preoccupied with clarifying their identity. *What kind of a man or woman am I becoming*, they were likely to wonder, *and how am I different from my mother or father?* They were asking, *Where can I find a few friends who will welcome me as I am and who will offer the familylike connections that I need [or never had]?* Or, *Can I love, and am I lovable?* These are relational questions, of course, and I could feel the discomfort of those in their twenties until they get answered. I found fear of rejection, loneliness, and the feeling that one might not fit. No wonder there were so many goings and comings among twenty-somethings, compelling a person toward one group or another, one friend or another. One needs to find a place, a people to whom one can belong.

The twenties are a time when one asks, *What will I do with my life? What is it that I really want in exchange for my life's labors?* Most denied that the key desire of life was for material wealth; the preference was for work that offered significance, a feeling of making a difference. Teaching, counseling, and work in the nonprofit sector were important possibilities. Of course, a bundle of folk said they were quite happy just to land a job—any passable job—that provides the income base for a reasonably secure life and some fun.

Twenty-somethings are becoming aware that they can no longer get away with irresponsible or unsocial behavior. Life patterns, habits, and personality quirks need adjustment if one is to get along. So the question, *what parts of me and my life need correction?* arises.

It is also not surprising that people in their twenties wrestle with the so-called *lordship* question: *Around what person or conviction will I organize my life?* Perhaps this is the mother of all questions (for every age, actually), but it reaches a point of great significance as one comes to the realization that the game of life is no longer the amateur game of the teen years. Now it is a serious matter with increasingly serious consequences, and one must identify an organizing principle that will bring the pieces of life into order. That *principle,* the Bible-embracing person believes, is really a person: Jesus Christ—His saving power, His call, His teachings.

———

What happens when twenty-somethings turn into thirty-somethings? The questions and issues begin to shift. The longer-range responsibilities of life begin to accumulate, and one's sense of personal freedom is compromised as more permanent relationships and commitments are made.

Since there is usually an expansion of responsibility and no expansion of time, thirty-somethings find themselves asking the question, *how do I prioritize the demands being made on my life?*

There are spouses to love and know more intimately, children who need endless amounts of attention, and jobs/careers that absorb energy. Homes must be maintained, bills paid, obligations to organizations met. Suddenly one must budget the yesses and the noes of life, and these decisions are not simply or easily made.

The career options of a person's life may have seemed clearer and simpler in the twenties. But now, in the thirties, one can begin to see that there are winners and losers, as well as also-rans (those who simply finish unnoticed in the middle of the pack). And the question forms: *How far can I go in fulfilling my sense of purpose?*

Because thirty-somethings are so busy getting life's routines established, there is little growing realization that one's primary community is changing. The friends of youth (and even the twenties) have split, gone off in different directions (some married, some single, many moved on to other parts of the world). And another question arises: *Who are the people with whom I know I walk through life?*

For many men, the thirties are the beginning of the onset of male loneliness. New male friendships are not easily made nor do they often measure up to the kind of friendships one used to enjoy. Old friends have drifted away; often, new acquaintances simply do not have the time to build the satisfying relationships that were part of the younger years.

Spiritual life changes for people in their thirties. The spiritual questions no longer center on the ideals of youth but on the realities of a life that is tough and unforgiving. There is little time for the long discussions with a mentor, the youth retreats and programs, the times of hanging out that marked earlier days. Now life's requirements offer little time for contemplation and spiritual revitalization. Most thirty-somethings who seek a spiritual component to life will tell you that words like *empty, tired, confused,* and *drifting* mingle in their thoughts in a way they never expected. Thus these questions materialize: *What does my spiritual life look like? Do I even have time for one?*

It's a quiet, nagging question that comes in moments when one feels that he or she has failed. Thirty-somethings are likely to see things in themselves they thought they might have overcome by now, simply by growing up. But things they once anticipated they would shake off *haven't* gone away. And thirty-somethings find themselves asking, *why am I not a better person?*

———

There are new questions that pop up in one's forties. The complexities of life further accelerate, and—and this is worrisome—we begin to recognize that we can no longer fob off our flaws and failures as youthfulness and inexperience. We are, as they say, *grown-up.* We are expected to handle the bumps and bruises of life with an unshakable courage. Panic and fear are for younger (and older?) people. But in one's forties, the expectation is that one is solid.

Still . . . there are questions. As I will illustrate in another part of this book, the question arises, *who was I as a child, and what powers back then influence the kind of person I am today?* We would have laughed at this question in our twenties, but now it becomes a rather serious one for more than a few.

Why do some people seem to be doing better than I? Why am I often disappointed in myself and others? Why are limitations beginning to outnumber options?

I believe the forties to be dangerous, uncharted waters for a lot of us. Lots of things begin to happen for which many of us are not prepared. Bodies change. Children become more independent, even begin to leave home. Marriages have to be readjusted to face new realities. Some of us begin to enjoy financial leverage; others of us begin to assume that we will never be materially secure. Some give up the fight to achieve lifelong goals and settle into a defensive posture of living. Others miss their youth and its seeming excitement so much that they try going backward to retrieve earlier pleasures.

Forty-somethings may ask, *why do I seem to face so many uncertainties?* But others may begin plotting a second life, a second career. *What can I do to make a greater contribution to my generation?* Or, *what would it take to pick up a whole new calling in life and do the thing I've always wanted to do?* If one listens carefully, he might hear the word *trapped* used in the questions that now arise.

A few wise forty-somethings may seek a ninety-day sabbatical. They will strip their lives down to bare metal and evaluate their life-journeys to this point. They'll take a hard look at their spiritual journeys, their personal relationships, their convictions about money and possessions, how they contribute their energies and resources. And when the assessment is over, they will have plotted a whole new course for the second half of life. A very exciting adventure for brave people.

———

Fifty-somethings would often prefer not to think about it, but the fact is that they have moved across life's middle. Now one finds him- or herself wondering how many years are left. The news of friends dying, marriages dissolving, and people moving to places of retirement increases. It can be a time for sober thinking.

John Dean of Watergate fame wrote:

My view [of my life] has been backward, not forward . . . and I have been dwelling on the trivial, on the insignificant too much. Time is running out and I must come to terms with my life. The days for fantasizing great achievements are gone. Ambitions and goals must be realistic if I want to avoid great disappointment at the end.[1]

So those in the fifties may ask, *why is time moving so fast?* Because it is *moving so fast.* It seems as if yesterday was Christmas, and tomorrow is Christmas. Go figure! We look at contemporaries and they suddenly look very old to us. Surely we have not aged that much!

Why is my body becoming unreliable? How do I deal with my failures and my successes? How can my spouse and I reinvigorate our relationship now that the children are gone? For those who haven't reached these questions yet, may I say, "Get ready!" Each will come at you, often without warning. It is worth getting a head start on them.

Who are these young people who want to replace me? It is a frightening moment when one discovers that younger people may know more than I, may be willing to work longer and harder than I am willing to work, and may be impatient for me to move over and give them the same chance to prove themselves that I once demanded.

What do I do with my doubts and fears? Will we have enough money for the retirement years if there are health problems and economic downturns? These questions loom in our fifties.

———

The sixty-year-old asks: *When do I stop doing the things that have always defined me? Why do I feel ignored by a large part of the younger population? Why am I curious about who is listed in the obituary column of the papers, how they died, and what kinds of lives they lived?*

The sixty-something wonders what is yet to be accomplished, and *do I have enough time to do all the things I've dreamed about in the past?* He or she may not want to admit it, but the question hovers, *who will be around me when I die?* And, if married, *which one of us will go first, and what is it like to say good-bye to someone with whom you have shared so many years of life?*

For more than a few, these are the years when doubts and fears may arise in quiet moments. *Are the things I've believed in capable of taking me to the end? Is there really life after death? What do I regret? And what are the chief satisfactions of these many years of living? What have I done that will outlive me?*

———

Perhaps the seventies and eighties blend together and share several kinds of questions. Now one is curious and asks these things: *Does anyone realize, or even care, who I once was? Is anyone aware that I once owned [or managed] a business, threw a mean curveball, taught school, possessed a beautiful solo voice, had an attractive face? Is my story important to anyone?*

How much of my life can I still control? they add. Some must stop driving. Others will have to surrender the administration of their finances to a younger person. Many will live in communities where most of life is scheduled for them.

Is there anything I can still contribute? Not everyone wants to sit or simply play. The body may be old, but some of us still want to make a difference. Can we?

Why this anger and irritability? Is God really there for me? Am I ready to face death? And when I die (how will it happen?), will I be missed, or will the news of my death bring relief?

Heaven? What is it like?

As a resilient person lays out his or her life and contemplates it from a long-range point of view, these are the questions for which one might want to prepare. If they have no answers, they create a fatigue in one's spirit. They slash away at vitality.

As I sit with forty senior friends and listen to them talk about their fondest memories, I see these questions in their eyes and hear them in their voices. And it challenges me, because I am just a few years from getting the same invitation (I hope) that Gail and I gave to them.

EIGHT

RESILIENT PEOPLE CULTIVATE CHRISTIAN CHARACTER

In his book *Soul-Making*, Allen Jones describes a visit to the Coptic Monastery of St. Macarius in the Egyptian desert. His host, Father Jeremiah, a bearded monk of indeterminate age, filled him full of stories of the desert fathers. Like this one.

One day, it is said, Saint Macarius, among the wisest of monks, was asked by a young man, "Abba, tell us about being a monk." Marcarius responded, "Ah! I'm not a monk myself, but I have seen them."

Having related this tale, Jones writes, Father Jeremiah then offered his own version, saying to Jones, "I am not *yet* a Christian, but I have seen them."[1]

Does it need to be said that the monk's words should not be analyzed theologically, but rather, experientially? "I am not *yet* a Christian" suggests a humility, a realization that life is more than promises and intentions. The phrase is about *becoming a person* who matches his words . . . maybe better yet, the words of Jesus. Younger people refer to this as *authenticity*.

I have this thought about resilient people. They are often more attuned to *process* than *position*.

The word *Christian* is often used to describe a personal experience in which one has declared that he has trusted in Jesus to forgive his sins and to receive the gift of eternal life. "When did you become a Christian?" someone asks. The answer is usually stated in terms of a date and place.

But when the word *Christian* is used to identify a process of spiritual development, it describes a life-journey in which one walks in the ways of Christ and gradually becomes more like Him in conduct and inner orientation. And this, of course, is the perspective out of which Father Jeremiah speaks when he says, "I am not yet a Christian, but I have seen them." The key word is *yet*, because he intends—through his personal growth—to become one. Process! He is unwilling to identify himself by words alone.

Resilient people think in terms of a big picture, and this is one of the things they think about and ask themselves as they look down the road of their journeys: *Am I becoming a Christian?*

More than anything, we're talking character, Christlike character, here. The kind of person I am becoming as a result of my choice to follow Jesus. In His invitation to people—"Come to [or "follow"] Me"—Jesus said, "Learn from Me." Translation: absorb My character by focusing on Me.

So what would people learn if they followed Him? A way of being. A way of seeing and hearing. A way of relating and doing business with other human beings. A way of seeing creation and the brokenness of life in the world. An invitation to action. To come to Jesus was to change life, piece by piece.

In his book *Seizing Your Divine Moment*, Erwin McManus writes of a day when he was speaking at a Christian retreat in Florida. His family had accompanied him on the trip. "My assignment," McManus relates, "was to call several thousand singles to a life of sacrifice as we basked in soothing tranquility."

During some free time, McManus and his ten-year-old son, Aaron, took a walk along the ocean. Suddenly he noted a disabled man on crutches, struggling to make his way to the water's edge to join other bathers. But because the sand was too unstable, the man fell and was unable to get up again. McManus admits that his instinct was to turn and walk in the opposite direction.

I know this instinct. It is the part of each of us that prefers not to get involved, not to face something that could be beyond our grasp. The temptation is to freeze, ignore it, hope that someone else will step up to the situation. Something in one's character goes into neutral, and self-interest threatens to trump self-sacrifice.

Not so with McManus's boy.

"My son stopped me," McManus says.

"I have to go help that man," the boy said.

McManus: "I could only look at him and say, 'Then go help him.'"

When the fallen man proved too heavy for a small boy to help, others quickly gathered around and offered the necessary strength. At first the child was distressed that he could not do it himself, but McManus said, "I explained to Aaron that his strength carried the man. It was because of him that others came to his aid."[2]

This is character in motion, best illustrated in the instincts of a ten-year-old. With apologies to Erwin McManus, whom I greatly admire, who in this particular story is the grown-up?

Character is a word that describes the default "me." The person I am over the long haul in life. The person who emerges in the most difficult, challenging moments. Character identifies the attitudes, convictions, and resulting behaviors that distinguish my life.

Let's put it another way: character is what people can expect of me in *most* situations. *Most*, I say, because all of us defy or betray our essential character from time to time. When we say "he acted out of character," we are noting either some exceptionally good or bad behavior that contrasts with what we have come to anticipate of a person. Character, then, is the deep current of what we are day after day after day.

The deep current within us out of which character arises must be monitored and, if necessary, redirected and rebuilt. Words like *growth*, *transformation*, and *maturity* are important to resilient people. True, they could become self-absorbed by this penchant for self-development (all virtues have a trap built into them), but let us concentrate on the strength side before we worry about the potential weakness.

We can all produce surface changes in life. The current concern about weight reduction is a good illustration. People adapt a diet and an exercise program, and for a few months they regain a weight level that pleases them. But unless they have revised their entire view of eating, they eventually migrate back to former ways and feel worse than before they began.

We often do the same with a habit we don't like. We turn over a new leaf—as they say—in a marriage relationship, or we reorder our ways of work. But the discouraging thing is that a few months later we find ourselves back to the "same ol' same ol.'"

Surface change usually doesn't work. It's only when one does a root canal (an apt metaphor, I think) on one's soul and rebuilds at the foundational level of life that real change happens. And this means that we're at character level.

People who are resilient believe that character is always changeable. Saint Teresa had this comment about character in the life of a sister in her convent and about character in her own life:

There is one sister in the community who has the knack of rubbing me the wrong way at every turn; her mannerisms, her ways of speaking, her character strike me as unlovable. But then she's a [sister]; God must love her dearly; so I am not going to let my natural dislike of her get the best of me.

Thus, I remind myself that [Christian] love is not a matter of feelings; it means doing things. I have determined to treat this sister as if she is the person I love best in the world. Every time I meet her, I pray for her, and I offer [thanks] to God for her virtues and her efforts. I feel certain that Jesus would like me to do this.[3]

This is what character transformation looks like. In the tradition of spiritual disciplines, there is an exercise called self-examen—the discipline of putting oneself under the microscope and seeing oneself as God might. You see Teresa doing it.

Few of us would argue that this is not important, but it's probably fair to say that not many of us make self-examen a regular discipline. George MacDonald (no relation) says:

Foolish is the man, and there are many such men, who would rid himself or his fellows of discomfort by setting the world right, by waging war on the evils around him, while he neglects that integral part of the world where lies his business, *his first business—namely his own character and conduct.*[4] (emphasis mine)

The practice of continuous repentance is a part of character development. It seems to me that the concept of repentance has been misunderstood and unfortunately applied to the occasional expression of deep regret over an unusually heinous sin. And, of course, this is something that is occasionally called for. But in the larger sense, repentance is that regular, sincere acknowledgment of all that is broken within me and which needs fixing. It is the expression of the humbled tax collector, of whom Jesus spoke, who was so distressed over his life that he felt unworthy to even enter the inner parts of the temple. Thus he stood, Jesus said, at a distance and prayed, "God be merciful to me a sinner" (Luke 18:13 KJV). Simple words but much in contrast to the Pharisee, who presumed his own innocence and thanked God that he was not like other people . . . like the tax collector, for example (v. 13).

Continuous repentance need not be a maudlin exercise of self-recrimination. We don't need to return to a "woe is me" time when there was an overage of words designed to strip one's sense of value in God's eyes. Rather, we're talking about a frank assessment of one's shortfalls, an acknowledgment before God of their existence, and a serious intention to correct the wrongs. Face it; name it; renounce it; replace it.

Then again, I have taken deliberate notice of men and women of my own generation whose paths I cross from time to time. There are few experiences more valuable than to sit in the shadow of a godly old man or woman, heroes of a kind, who carry the scars and marks of a long-lived faith. Give me a crack at them, and I'll find a hundred questions to ask so that I can get to the root of their character. Who were their heroes? Where were the life-building crises? What have been the enduring principles of life? Regrets? Delights? Hopes and dreams?

Paul wrote, "Join with others in following my example, brothers, and take note of those who live according to the pattern we gave you . . . our citizenship is in heaven" (Phil. 3:17, 20).

I'm not confident that character can be changed without a vision of what's possible. What kind of a man do I wish to be in five years? Better, where could my life more powerfully emulate Jesus in five years? Give me three or four patterns of behavior or thought that need strengthening.

Presently, I'm working on patience, one of the qualities the Bible calls a "fruit of the Spirit" (Gal. 5:22). I used to think of myself as a patient man, but I'm not so sure now. I find a flicker of irritability rising in me when the line at the post office is too long, when everyone else decided to clog up the interstate at the same time I wanted to drive it, when someone sends me an e-mail file that takes ten minutes to download. I have a suspicion that these bits of impatience really echo other aspects—maybe more significant aspects—of my life that I refuse to face. So when I'm standing in the post office line and feel this impatience, I push myself to stop and think about my idiotic, immature reaction. Why am I upset because I'm going to lose four or more minutes in my schedule? What's the deeper impatience? Where's the anger coming from?

The moment in the line becomes a tutorial for my character. There will be moments ahead when patience will be needed for far greater issues than this one. Learn patience here so that you will have it then.

Character is developed—for believers, anyway—when we let the Scripture inform us. We are what we permit to enter the deepest parts of our soul. A steady diet of television, cheap publications, and shallow literature will make us dreadfully inadequate people. A daily exposure to the Scripture and to literature that focuses on Scripture is a necessary part of the diet.

The resilient person who would build Christian character understands the importance of carefully considered values that spring from a life grounded in Scripture—a regular and serious application of the Holy Word.

Once I was stranded in Hong Kong, having been bounced (reason: overbooking) from a flight on Singapore Airlines. The airline people politely told me that there was no chance of leaving for at least two days. I booked a hotel room for the first night and returned to the airport the next day. Hour after hour I sat, hoping that a seat would open up on some flight and that I'd be given a boarding pass so I could get home.

Seated next to me was a man who was clearly accustomed to international travel. He shared my predicament. Suddenly, he got up and approached the gate agent. I could tell that their conversation was more than a little vigorous. And when he returned, he was holding a boarding pass.

"Now let me tell you how it works," he said. "I went over there. I used every bit of profanity I know; I told him what I thought of his airline and that I'd never fly it again. I demanded a seat on this next flight, and I got it." He flaunted his boarding pass. And then he said, "So if you go over there and do the same thing, you might get lucky."

I approached the same gate agent and said, "Sir, I've been told that if I get real mean and nasty, it's possible you'll give me a boarding pass. Now, frankly, I'm not that kind of a guy. I don't believe in belittling people and swearing at them. Nevertheless, I'd really like to get home. So, do you think you could help me out?"

He said, "I'll see." I returned to my seat with optimism. I expected to be able to say to my friend, "There's another, a *better*, way to get things done." And when this happened, he'd probably express admiration for my character and ask me about my faith. I really did expect this.

The conclusion of the matter was that my comrade boarded the flight and headed home. I spent the next day and a half in Hong Kong. The moral of the story: *character doesn't always result in the kind of success one wants.* We don't develop character because it brings success; we develop it because it is the right way, the God-pleasing way to live. One lives by the Bible whether or not things turn out the convenient way.

When the Coptic monk tells Allen Jones, "I am not *yet* a Christian, but I have seen them," he reveals the front edge of his character. *Yet,* I said, is the operational word. It reminds us that he's growing. He has an objective in mind: to be fully formed in the Christlike way. And that means character building. Resilient people believe this.

NINE

RESILIENT PEOPLE LISTEN FOR A CALL FROM GOD

My editor at *Leadership Journal,* for which I have regularly written over the past years, recently asked me to write on the subject of life-calling. I gave the subject as much thought as I could and then wrote my article. But after I had sent the piece off, I found myself restless. "When," I asked, "was I last called?"

We sometimes use the language of "leading" to describe what we think are God's nudges in daily life. "I felt God *leading* me to give him a call," we might say.

But a call is different. It describes a summons to a way of life, a responsibility, a long-term task. It is not just a call to some form of paid ministry or missionary life, although it could be that. But there is something deeper, more expansive to the subject of calling. It is an acknowledgment that one is accountable to God for the discharge of his life's duties.

My call—to be a pastor (and I believe a preacher and writer)—is an old story. It goes back to my childhood. It's an old call, if you please. And writing the article made me yearn for a new call. And I began to pray each day, "God, give me a fresh calling."

Soon after I began praying like this, I traveled to Germany to speak at a series of pastors' conferences. Each day I told stories and tried to reduce ministry leadership to some useful principles. I often gave illustrations of places where I'd succeeded or failed.

At the end of each day I would be approached by young German pastors, some of whom would say to me, "You talk to us like a father."

"What do you mean?" I'd ask.

"The old German pastors talk to us like professors. But you talk like a father. You tell us your stories, and you are not afraid to tell us where you have struggled." *That's all I've got of interest: my struggles,* I thought to myself.

A few days after I returned from Europe, I flew to California to speak at another leadership conference. At the end of the weekend, the conference leader stepped to the front to thank me. He told the audience, "All weekend there have been times when I found myself on the edge of tears. But not because Gordon is that bad of a speaker, but because *he talks to us like a father,* and so many of us feel fatherless."

In that moment I felt God whisper, *You've got your call. Be a father to a younger generation. Speak like a father; talk to younger men and women like one; write like one.* So I now have this fresh call.

People who are resilient live by the gravitational pull of a call. They believe that God's hand is upon their lives and that they must respond to that call. Thus, resilient people reflect on questions such as, *what path should my life be taking, and what should I be doing with the resources and sensitivities with which God has blessed me?* They resonate with Paul when he spoke in Acts 26 of that "vision from heaven" to which he remained obedient to the end of his life (v. 19).

Eighty-five-year-old Caleb was engaging in big-picture thinking when he looked back upon his life and said, "I . . . followed the LORD my God wholeheartedly" (Josh. 14:8). He was a called man!

I believe that big-picture thinking—at least for the Bible believer—demands a sense of *call.* Heaven imprints the heart of a person with a compelling destiny that provides meaning and focus to life.

There must be in most people a deep instinct to hear such a call, to feel that we can align our lives with a higher sense of purpose than just the routines of daily living. I suspect that this is one of the reasons behind the success of Rick Warren's book *The Purpose Driven Life*. In a reflective moment one sees the book with its compelling title on the bookshelf of an airport store and purchases it. Why? Because we yearn to get caught up in something bigger than we are.

German philosopher Friedrich Schleiermacher knew that desire when he said, "My calling and my friends, those are the two hinges on which my life turns."

Turn in almost any direction as you walk through the Bible, and you will find a "call story." It will describe how some person—often living in obscurity—was overcome with a compelling message from heaven that redirected life into something purposeful. At first glance, most of the call stories appear in the context of a religious vocation: a call to be a prophet or an apostle, for example, or a call to be pastor or king.

But then you come across a call story like the one that features Bezalel and Oholiab, two builders among the Hebrews who were delivered out of Egypt. God speaks to Moses about the two men:

> "I have chosen Bezalel . . . and I have filled him with the Spirit of God, with skill, ability and knowledge in all kinds of crafts—to make artistic designs for work in gold, silver and bronze, to cut and set stones, to work in wood, and to engage in all kinds of craftsmanship. Moreover, I have appointed Oholiab . . . to help him." (Ex. 31:2–6)

These two men sound like everyday folks to me, the kind I often see during breakfast at the Egg Shell Restaurant down the road from where we live in New Hampshire. They arrive in their pickups, which have snowplows on the front, ladders bungee corded to a rack over the cab, and large chrome toolboxes fitted in the bed. They come in, shed battered old L. L. Bean parkas, and gather around tables to drink coffee together before heading out for the construction site. You've seen these kinds of guys, I'm sure. Bezalel and Oholiab would fit well at their table, and they were *called* men.

Esther comes to mind when I think of call stories. Here is a young woman caught up in an ancient practice by which a despot adds to his harem. But when a situation arises that smells like ethnic cleansing for an entire generation of Jews, Esther is uniquely positioned to initiate an intervention. "Do not think that because you are in the king's house you alone of all the Jews will escape," her mentor (and probably uncle) Mordecai wrote her (Est. 4:13).

> "For if you remain silent at this time, relief and deliverance for the Jews will arise from another place, but you and your father's family will perish. And who knows but that you have come to royal position for such a time as this?" (v. 14)

There are other examples of call stories where the efforts are not religious in a formal sense. Nehemiah the wall builder, Daniel the government man in Babylon, and Luke, a first-century physician: they're all *called* people.

So it would be hard to read through the Bible and not conclude that *call* is a significant transaction between God and people who believe that He is involved in earthly matters. Thus, strategic thinking will have to begin here: *What do I hear God saying about the direction of my life and its contribution?*

The biblical calls had several commonalities. First, in one way or another, they all originated in one of the Holy Three. God the Father *called* Abraham, Moses, Isaiah, and Amos (to name a few). Jesus *called* twelve men to "be with him" (Mark 3:14), and then sent them out to spread the faith among the nations. The Holy Spirit *called* Saul and Barnabas and others to apostolic opportunity. No one in the Bible called him- or herself.

Biblical calls were also quite unpredictable. Gideon, for example, responded to his call, "How can I save Israel? My clan is the weakest in Manasseh, and I am the least in my family" (Judg. 6:15). Why did God call David? Or Jeremiah? And why, for heaven's sake, Simon Peter? Then add to the list the improbable call to Saul of Tarsus, who would later recollect, "[At the time of my call] I was . . . a blasphemer and a persecutor and a violent man" (1 Tim. 1:13)?

When Saint Francis was asked why God called him, he was reflecting on unpredictability when he said, "God picks the weakest, the smallest, the meanest of men on the face of the earth, and he uses them."

There's another common point in most of these call stories: they often focused on mind-boggling, seemingly impossible objectives. Build a boat, Noah; lead people out of Egypt, Moses; face down a wicked king, Elijah; preach to Gentiles, Paul. But such calls were so challenging that they often brought things out of a person that he or she never knew was there.

Finally, each biblical call was unique. No call seemed like any other. The circumstances of the call, the nature of the call, the expectations of the call, all customized. When God wanted a word said or a people led, He mandated a person to make it happen in an unprecedented way. Each who was called learned to trust the One who did the calling, and out of the trust found courage, wisdom, and direction.

Calls were not classified ads, so that anyone could volunteer. Persons, sometimes strange persons, were selected, while others, seemingly more worthy and capable, were not. There was only *one* Moses, in spite of what Miriam and Aaron dared to think the day they asked, "Hasn't [God] also spoken through us?" (Num. 12:2). There was only one Esther, one John the Baptizer, one Simon Peter.

These not-so-novel observations are worth repeating constantly, for they form a foundation for dignifying the Christian life and giving it a great sense of meaning.

My own call has been that of a preacher and a pastor, and I have lived my life under that discipline. Looking back, the call seems to have emerged in a family conspiracy in which my mother and grandmother prayed fervently that God would raise up a preacher in their family. That apparently was me. How (or why) God merged His choice with the prayers of two women is a mystery to me. But their role of prayer is part of the story.

In my second year of life, two military aircraft collided over our home and showered fuel and flaming debris over our neighborhood. I was in our backyard in the one place that escaped the falling wreckage of the collision. That my life was spared was indeed a mystery, perhaps a miracle. Three years later, a similar incident occurred when I nearly drowned. Thus the family story: that my life had been preserved by God for purposes which only He knew and would only reveal later on.

"Be very careful," my mother would say. "You dare never say no to God. Should you choose to do anything else but what God calls you to do, you'll be a sad person all of your life." Looking back, I regard remarks such as these as a bit over the top. But, again, they're part of the story.

Throughout the years of my childhood and even into my teen years I was romanced by the idea of pastoral life. When other boys dreamed of driving fire trucks and playing professional baseball, I dreamed of preaching the Bible and leading people to Jesus. A one-time babysitter tells me that, at the age of four, I loved playing "worship service," in which she was the congregant and I was the pastor.

As a teenager, I gained a love for words, for public speaking, for leadership. Men and women in ministry took an interest in me and commented that they saw potential in me to do pastoral work. The formation of a bundle of gifts began to evidence itself. Furthermore, my own heart soared when I listened to people challenge me in the direction of kingdom activity. I could see myself in a pulpit or doing missionary work. Nothing else was quite so interesting.

Midway through my college years, at a low point in my spiritual journey, I succumbed to an impulse to try and join the Air Force and fly jets. I went to the Air Force recruiting center to take the required physical examination. "You're color-confused," a doctor said as he examined my eyes. "You can't distinguish certain colors well enough to qualify as a pilot. You'll never fly for the Air Force!" My minirebellion against God's call was squashed.

As I left the recruiting center I thought I heard a bit of laughter from heaven, as if God was saying, "Did you really think you could get away from your call that easily?" And once more I submitted to what seemed to be the inevitable—I was destined to serve God.

When I met my wife, Gail, we fell in love quickly and easily, because both of us had a similar sense of a desire to serve Jesus in what was referred to as a "full-time" way. Soon the call to ministry became more specified, and I realized with the help of others that my "instincts" (gifts?) were those of a pastor—not an administrator, not an evangelist, not a missionary.

And now all these years of adult life have passed, and with few exceptions, there has never been a time when I have not enjoyed life from a pastoral perspective: being there for people in their tough moments, encouraging them to be strong in the Lord, challenging them to personal growth in Christlikeness, helping them discern *their* calls and giftedness. Even though I no longer have the day-to-day responsibility for a congregation, I still function as a pastor in my work, and it remains just as satisfying.

You could label this a "call story." Every *called* person has one. A call story is a history of "whispered words and events" that capture the soul and make one aware that God is speaking.

For some of us the call story is kind of dramatic. In one forceful moment there is a sense of conviction that God has spoken and directed. One is never again the same after this.

For others, like myself, the call is like a continual dripping: it just beats on you until you capitulate and say, "OK, OK!" And I'm thankful that I did.

Once one is called, financial security, location, notoriety, applause, and power become increasingly less important. Obedience becomes the primary issue. Let others feel free to build fortunes and empires; the call binds one to surrender him- or herself to the will of God. I fear this sounds schlocky, but it's been the perspective of called people for centuries now.

A call, it seems to me, comes about in several ways.

First: *heaven speaks!* The ways of speaking? Many and varied. But there is a moment of certainty that God has put His hand upon a person and nudged that individual toward a particular people, theme, or function.

When Eric Liddle, in *Chariots of Fire,* said to his sister, "When I run, I feel God's pleasure," he provoked a mysterious thought. He put his finger on a hard-to-explain dimension of *call.* When one lives obediently in the center of a call, one feels God's pleasure; one knows a strange joy.

During the first week of the 9/11 tragedy, Gail and I worked alongside of Salvation Army officers at ground zero. Each day we poured ourselves into the rescue effort, doing whatever needed to be done. We were there because we'd both felt a strong sense of God's leading to go there and do what we could. More than once I would embrace Gail and whisper into her ear, "I was made for this. We belong here."

Second, the genuineness of a call is usually (not always, but usually) confirmed by others who discern the unique work of God's Spirit in a particular person. People who know us well watch, and they volunteer comments such as, "You glow when you're doing that." "You are at your best when you . . ." "You seem so natural when you're . . ."

When Gail heard me make a first attempt at preaching (not long after we'd met) she put her arms around me, kissed me, and whispered, "God gave me a vision tonight that He intends for you to become a good preacher." I've often thought that her comment, more than any other single thing, gave me the final confidence I needed to pursue preaching (and later writing) as my vocation.

A third part of the authentic call seems to be giftedness. There are some romantic (and probably true) stories of calls where a person started off with no specific capacities at all. But that is probably rare. With a call comes giftedness—that mysterious empowerment of capability and spirit that God visits upon the "callee." When such people are in alignment with their calls, they fairly soar. Something powerful happens, and we the observers are all left in amazement.

As Saint Francis thought strategically, he had his heart awakened to the poor. "Go towards the poor," he heard God say in several different ways: in his heart, through his friends, from inescapable confrontations with lepers. The pope tried to make him an administrator, a builder of buildings, a functionary in the hierarchy. But he refused this pressure, because his instinct was tuned to the cry of the poor. And all who had known him as the rather frivolous son of a middle-class cloth dealer marveled at the transformation in his life. Intuitively, he knew just what to do when he engaged the poor.

Finally, there are the results themselves. As I do what I do, does the world around me become a bit better of a place? Are people encouraged by my presence? Does an institution or a business become a better place to work because of my contribution? Do I add something to the human equation in my home, at my job, in my neighborhood, in my church?

Saint Patrick had a dream. In the dream, Irish people were saying, "We appeal to you, holy servant boy, to come and walk among us." For

Patrick it was a call, and he was obedient. He combed the Irish countryside, bearing witness to chiefs and kings. An entire nation began its journey to Christian conversion. To borrow words from Thomas Cahill, the long-term result of Patrick's call was national transformation, and the Irish monks in turn *"saved civilization."*

Let us be frank: men and women have obeyed God's call and become martyrs. Others have undertaken unspeakably difficult and discouraging tasks and barely survived. Many more have lived the relatively common life between home and job. They hammer nails, sell widgets, create software, or fix things. But in the process they make a difference in the existence of the people around them. And they, too, are called.

TEN

RESILIENT PEOPLE ARE CONFIDENT IN THEIR GIFTEDNESS

It is almost twenty years now since we said good-bye to Lynn. At the age of twenty-nine, Lynn died of Hodgkin's disease. I'm confident that she lives in heaven today, but I also see her, in another sense, living in two people, our son and our daughter.

We met Lynn when she was a young teenager. We had asked her to stay with our children on a few occasions when we had to be involved together at the church. It didn't take long to note that when Lynn was in charge (unlike with most other babysitters), Mark and Kristy always got to bed on time. The house was always clean and peaceful when we got home. And if one of the children (it's hard to admit this) misbehaved, Lynn was careful to tell us.

One day Lynn said, "I want to support what you are doing. Here's my deal. If you'll give me a monthly calendar of all the times when you need my help with the children, I'll be available. But there's one stipulation: I will not take any pay for what I do."

We protested this stipulation but discovered that Lynn could be stubborn about such things.

For the next three to four years, Lynn played a major role in our family life. Our children benefited (as did their parents) from the continuity of watch care whenever it was necessary for Gail and me to be away. We enjoyed the security of knowing that our children were in the company of someone who believed as we did in the discipleship of children. It was a perfect fit, a gift, we thought, from God.

The day came when we moved from the Midwest to New England, and the four of us had to say good-bye to Lynn. Naturally, we kept in close touch, and Lynn came to visit our home in Lexington, Massachusetts, on many occasions.

When Lynn graduated from college, she committed herself to raising foster children from abusive homes. The social service arm of the State of Illinois came to trust her as one to whom they could entrust some of their most serious cases of child abuse and neglect. There were always five or more children under Lynn's care, and many of them went on to live normal lives as a result of her remarkable devotion to them.

I'm not sure where you'd go in the Bible to find the exact name for it, but Lynn had a gift. Could it be called a *nurturing* gift? Whatever you wish to call it (some might call it the gift of mercy), it was in perfect alignment with her sense of call to invest in children.

We liked to think that Lynn first heard her call in our home. And we like to think that we were among the first to see and affirm the remarkable gift of nurturing that she possessed. Lynn never birthed a child of her own. But she raised many children born to other mothers.

Christian people who think big picture believe in giftedness. They study the Scriptures and discover the stories of men and women who received a gracious capacity from God to achieve particular things.

In the Old Testament you can see gifts of leadership (Moses), gifts of expression (David), gifts of wisdom (Solomon), and gifts of prophetic confrontation (Elijah comes to mind). There were artistic gifts, managerial gifts, and serving gifts.

The gifts were not seen only in competencies (things one does) but also in character and personality (the ability to influence). Here and there, men and women emerged who brought just the right perspective to the situation so that the purposes of God were advanced.

There have been a zillion books on *spiritual gifts*. It's possible that everything of value has been said on the subject. Sometimes I fear that the "doctrine" of spiritual gifts has been sliced and diced so intricately that some of us could miss the point. Some take the lists of gifts in the New Testament books and try to cram every possibility of human ingenuity into the limited set of categories. But what if those are just samples of gifts or the ones the writer had in mind on the day that the material was written?

What if "gift" isn't as much a specific category of activity, but a word meant to describe the way God wishes for each of His people to fit in functionally with everyone else.

Paul introduced the subject of giftedness to the Ephesians by stating that Jesus gave gifts to the family of God. His brief list sounds more like the leadership categories that a church might need: apostles and prophets, pastors, teachers, and evangelists. Certainly he could have enlarged that list considerably. Heaven help the church if it doesn't have more gifted people than merely those five.

What I think may be more important is the reasons for the "gifts" that Jesus gave. Among the reasons: that people be trained (coached) to do the work of God; that the family of God might be strengthened; that everyone might grow up to be like Jesus; and that we not become victims of mistruth and seductive false voices.

To the Roman Christians Paul spoke of giftedness in terms of functions, such as preaching, serving, encouraging, giving, leadership, and mercy. With the Corinthians Paul talked about other gifts: wisdom, healing, discernment, and tongues of praise.

It's a pretty diverse list, and people have worked hard to put it all in clear categories. What if they are actually wasting their time trying to make everything fit so nicely? What if this—as I said before—is all a matter of sampling?

I would like to propose that we cease trying to distinguish between talents, skills, and gifts and recognize at the highest possible level that all of these competencies are heaven-sent. Our dear friend Lynn's ability to *mother* children was a gift. Think of the beneficiaries. Our children benefited from a consistency of supervision and care. Gail and I benefited knowing that our children were getting the best oversight possible. The people of our church benefited from the availability of their pastor and his wife. One person using her unique sense of call and giftedness leveraged a blessing that touched a multitude of people.

People who think big picture recognize that there are a thousand different efforts to which they might make a contribution. But they also know that there are only a few of those efforts to which they can make a maximized contribution on the basis of their giftedness.

Many years ago I came to a couple of realizations about myself. One was that virtually everything there was to do fascinated me. There was hardly any effort in the church that I did not find immediately interesting. Thus it was easy for me to say yes to everything and become so swamped with commitments and promises made that I was exhausted and producing relatively little.

This meant that I had to learn to say some strategic noes to things that looked fascinating and challenging. And that meant living with occasional disappointment.

The second thing I learned was about the core of my job as a pastor. There were tasks I was expected to undertake, but that did not mean that I was equally gifted in the doing of each of them.

I can cast a vision; I'm a visionary. I can preach and write; I'm a communicator. I can encourage people; I'm a people builder. In these areas I am capable—if God's power is upon my life—of effective pastoral leadership.

But my role also demands administrative activities. I'm expected to do some counseling. And I'm expected to engage in organizing work. But with these three I have exited from the core of my gifts. In order to do these, I have to work very hard and use far more time and energy than I have to expend when I am doing the things listed in the previous paragraph.

One can drive a car from New York to San Francisco in any of four or five speeds indicated on the gear shift. But the drive is best done in gears meant for speed and fuel economy. To drive the distance in second gear would mean engine wear, fuel waste, and slow speeds.

In my life there are things—administration is one of them—that I must do in second gear. And there are things I can do in overdrive. Perhaps preaching is among those. Obviously I must find a way to slough off the low-gear activities and embrace the overdrive ones, because they are in the core of my giftedness.

Resilient people identify those particular functions and qualities of being that are clearly in the gift zone. It is not really that hard to do.

First, it could be reasonably assumed that—in most cases—a sense of clear call will be matched by giftedness. The two will usually go together. I have to qualify my statement, because everyone, sooner or later, meets someone who appears to defy the combination. They are called but seemingly not gifted (as far as we can see), but they get the job done anyway.

In Simon Peter's case, it would have been hard to see the convergence of call and gift in his first months with Jesus. His behavior seems impulsive, occasionally defiant. Later, when he shows himself to be a gifted leader in the church's early days, we see that the earlier behavior needed to be contained and crafted. And the impulsive Simon of disciple days became the quick-decision maker in apostle days.

Second, a gift will be evidenced by a certain naturalness in our conduct. Our son-in-law, Tom, is a remarkably gifted furniture craftsman. Sometimes it seems that all he has to do is look at a piece of maple or oak or mahogany, and it becomes exactly what he had in mind. In a hundred years I could not accomplish what he seems to do in a day when it comes to working with wood. It's clear to me that God gave Tom an eye, an imagination, and a dexterity that makes beautiful works of art that produce a living for his family.

Third, giftedness gets results. Things change in the hands of a gifted person. Organizations come together under the direction of those who are gifted in organizing. People are healed when someone has the gift of diagnosis. Victims are defended when someone brims with the gift of compassion.

Resilient people who think in big-picture terms carefully define their core of giftedness. Most of us will discover that there are three or four competencies to which we gravitate. We can tell stories of how we awakened to those competencies, but even we ourselves are hard pressed to explain why it is this and not that. All we know is that there is a mysterious fervor within us that rises and bubbles when we are in the center of the gift zone.

Dick Reckard was a member of the congregation at Grace Chapel, Lexington, Massachusetts. In the earliest days of the church's life, he served as superintendent of the Sunday school (now a fairly outdated term). As the church and its Christian Education program grew, the systems became increasingly sophisticated. And there came a moment when Dick had to admit that it was all bigger than him, and he would have to step out of the job. He could have held on to the job and become an obstacle in the way of growth, but he had the courage and foresight not to put himself first, but to hand the task on to more capable people.

The next thing I knew, Dick Reckard had taken on a new responsibility: showing up at Grace Chapel at ten o'clock every evening (six nights a week) to tour the buildings and make sure that every door was secure, every light turned off, and the heating system working. He lived exactly one mile from the church and—apart from the harshest weather conditions—walked from his home to the church each evening.

Those of us who were at church night after night became accustomed to seeing Dick make the rounds. When he showed up, we knew it was time to vacate the premises. The buildings were locking down. As Dick walked the halls and poked his head into each room, he would always—no exceptions—have a cheery word, a faithful "good night" for every person he encountered. Occasionally he would come across someone who was upset because a meeting had not gone well or he'd received a difficult piece of news.

That was Dick's cue to stop for a moment and talk . . . and pray. Many were the stories I heard of people whose day was rescued in the very final moments because they bumped into Dick Reckard, and he had a word of cheer for them.

Find a biblical word that combines that set of responsibilities into a gift. Encouragement? Mercy? Perhaps. Helps or serving? OK. I'm not sure that it's that important to name Dick Reckard's gifts. He was just faithful, doing what he felt most natural doing. Doing what got results and multiplied into blessing for lots of people.

After Dick went to heaven, it was impossible to find someone to take his place. As I recall, the church added many thousands of dollars to its budget to pay a person to do what Dick did: lock down the church. But there were no more stories of peoples' lives being touched as they made their way to their cars. Apparently, whatever the gift was, it died with him.

ELEVEN

RESILIENT PEOPLE LIVE GENEROUS LIVES

In almost everything I have written through the years, I have managed at least once to quote my hero, nineteenth-century Anglican priest Charles Simeon. One evening, when he was entertaining some of his closest friends, he said to them:

> I love to view all my Christian friends as fuel. Having gathered you all together at my hearth, I warm myself at your fire, and find my Christian love burns and glows.

In younger days of my life, I could not have made such a statement. Today I could. The Christian friends with whom Gail and I have been blessed are—along with our immediate family—our greatest treasure. Take away everything else, but leave our family and our special friends.

It is difficult to write these words, because I buried one of these closest friends just yesterday. His name? Al Napolitano. I have known him for more than thirty years. He was a man who was totally comfortable with himself, without guile, a man who loved God. In the days just before he died, we sat together and talked, man to man. Knowing that life was measured in mere days, there was no shame in holding each other's hand for an hour as we reflected on the memories of special times spent together. We talked openly about dying, and I was powerfully moved by his calmness. No fear, no anger. Just a calm readiness to enter into Jesus' presence.

Al was almost eighty when he left us. He was one of the most resilient men I've ever known. He loved taking pictures with his camera. He was active on his computer, sending and receiving e-mail. He was an avid reader, and we were constantly trading book titles as well as the books themselves. In the company of two other special friends, we flew to Switzerland two years ago and walked the Alpine wander-wegs for eight days.

Al was the first of a circle of my personal friends to die. Almost all of them were there yesterday and stood together at his grave with Lena, his wife. We grieved together and shed sweet tears. As I looked at each of the men and women in that group, I was suddenly struck with a powerful insight. While they had many things in common, there was one thing that stood out above all: *Every person in that circle has chosen to live generously.*

And that is a major marker in the big picture of resilient people: *They are, by intention, generous people.*

Al Napolitano had been a controller of a Boston-based business for twenty-seven years. When he reached his sixty-fifth year, he stepped down from his position and gave himself and his financial expertise to several nonprofit organizations in the Boston area. On Mondays he could be found at his church, supervising the counting of offerings. At other times he would be there to oversee audits and the compilation of financial reports that went to the congregation and to the lay leadership. Al's signature on any report was the ultimate sign of reliability.

At other times during the week, he could be found at the offices of Vision New England, a large interchurch agency that provides support and training for New England churches. There was nothing too small or too large. Al was willing to do whatever was needed for any effort that was going to make life better for someone. He never complained; he never whined; he never sought recognition or reward.

Perhaps this is why so many people loved and revered my friend Al. He asked for nothing but was prepared to give everything.

At the graveside stood another friend, Joanna Mockler, who lost her husband ten years ago. She, too, is a person whose entire life is marked with generosity. A considerable amount of her time is invested in the boards of two major world-renown Christian organizations. But the larger proportion of her time is spent in the discharge of one of her more remarkable spiritual gifts, the gift of prayer and faith.

When Joanna agrees to pray for you, you can expect an avalanche of prayer, and you can expect frequent contact as she searches out the way God may be responding to her intercession. Over the years of my Christian journey, I have heard countless people talk about prayer, but I have met only a relative few who mean what they say and do it at a level of intensity and depth that causes you to feel that you are in the company of a saint. Joanna Mockler is one of these.

(Big) Al MacLeod—all six and a half feet of him—was at the graveside too. He spent much of his career in strategic long-range planning for a major defense contractor. Often when we would talk in those days, he would say to me, "Someday I'm going to step away from all of this stuff, and I'm going to start giving back." He would dream aloud of applying his managerial skills to the running of a small nonprofit organization. And so we waited to see when and how that dream would come true.

Then came September 11, 2001. Spending the first week at ground zero with the Salvation Army gave me an idea. What if a hand-picked group of people could be trained and prepared to come alongside Salvation Army officers in the event of another major disaster in our country? I began to think of something akin to the National Guard, people prepared and prepositioned to spring into action when the call was sounded.

When I shared my dream with MacLeod, he was an intent listener. Coming from a military background, he knew exactly what I had in mind. Soon after, I proposed the idea to Salvation Army leaders, and they were romanced by the thought. It wasn't long before an introduction brought my friend Al together with the territorial commander of the Salvation Army in New England. The connection became so solid that it was best for me to get out of the way.

Before long Al was using every ounce of his career experience to create a disaster response plan that the Salvation Army in the Northeast would adopt. Today Al has an office in Boston, where he is constantly tweaking and reinforcing a plan of operation that could someday eventuate in the saving of countless lives. He even has a blue Salvation Army uniform that fits him. Where they found one his size, I have no idea.

Elsewhere I have written of others of my friends (very special friends) who stood at the graveside yesterday; these are just three of them: two very much in daily motion, the third now at home with Jesus, where recognition for the generous life abounds.

What marks all of my friends is generosity. Every one of them is up to his or her ears in serving the kingdom of God. That, I think, is the great commonality in our friendship.

The big picture of a resilient person is not complete without the component of generosity. Speaking of character, giftedness, life-direction, none of it hangs together until the generous piece is put into place. Generosity, you see, is the authenticating symbol of resilience, and it is the antithesis of a life trapped in materialism, self-centeredness, and an obsession with pleasure.

A long time ago I dropped the word *retirement* out of my vocabulary. I don't believe in it. In the aging process, slowing up in tandem with one's diminishing strength might be a necessity. But retirement suggests, at least to me, a transition from activity to inactivity, from giving to taking. Where in the Scriptures does one find permission to do that? We are called, *at all times of our lives,* to be generous with our time.

Most people think of generosity in terms of the almighty dollar. But generosity is a much larger issue than just money. We are talking about a way of life that begins with this question: *What of me can be shared, given away?*

Once I was in South Africa, and we were driving by an open field where there were small groups of homeless men sitting around fires. "What do you think they talk about?" I asked my host.

"No idea," he responded. "But I can tell you this. No man in that circle starves or goes without. If you approached that circle, you'd be offered something to sit on, something to drink, something to eat. No matter how little they have, a portion would be shared with you."

That's a provocative thought, I said to myself. I don't know that this could be said about most people of contrasting wealth who like to separate themselves from anyone who is not quite like them. But why should I be surprised? Every statistic, every social observation suggests that, pound for pound, the poor are far more generous than we who are the comparative wealthy.

So what does it mean to be generous? And generous with what? *With what one can do.*

"May the Lord show mercy to the household of Onesiphorus," Paul wrote, "because he often refreshed me and was not ashamed of my chains. On the contrary, when he was in Rome, he searched hard for me until he found me. May the Lord grant that he will find mercy from the Lord on that day! You know very well in how many ways he helped me in Ephesus" (2 Tim. 1:16–18). Wouldn't you love to know a man about whom it is said, "He often refreshed me"? How about this kind of person:

> Greet Priscilla and Aquila, my fellow workers in Christ Jesus. They risked their lives for me. Not only I but all the churches of the Gentiles are grateful to them. (Rom. 16:3–4)

This is the same couple that received a young man named Apollos into their home and coached him into maturity. "They risked their lives"; that's pretty strong language. I wonder what's behind that?

Of Timothy himself, Paul wrote, "I have no one else like him, who takes a genuine interest in your welfare. For everyone looks out for his own interests, not those of Jesus Christ" (Phil. 2:20–21).

I read these words and am reminded of my friends. This spirit of generosity—the giving of self—is not dead. It can be found in the lives of resilient people.

Again, generous with what? *With what one is.*

Is there a better name in the Bible than the name *Barnabas*? Originally, he was known as Joseph, but among the early believers the name *Barnabas* fit him better, since the name (Bar, son of; nabas, encouragement) translates "son of encouragement." And that's exactly what the man was: encouragement personified. Wherever he was, people were lifted to new levels. It was Barnabas whom we have to thank for the apostolic ministry of Paul. When the early church could not bring itself to believe in the authenticity of his conversion, it was Barnabas who took the risk and welcomed him into personal friendship. Later Barnabas would introduce Paul to the church at Antioch. And after that he would accompany him on his first apostolic efforts.

The last we hear of Barnabas concerns his defense of John Mark, a failed young man who needed a second chance. Apparently Barnabas's generous spirit could be touched. Ironically, Barnabas broke from Paul in order to support the younger man. I tell you, this was a very generous man.

Mary of Bethany was a generous woman. Not only because she poured an expensive spice over the head and feet of Jesus, but because she understood the sorrow that was gathering in His heart. When others ignored the poignancy of the approaching moment of His death, she was there to connect with Him, to let Him know of her friendship and gratitude. Of all the people who could have provided support for Jesus in those worst of hours, it was only Mary who was in touch with reality and who did something about it. I call that generosity.

Generous with what, you say? *With what one has.*

When you start searching the Scriptures for generosity of the financial kind, there is a rather ironic conclusion. The people most generous with their money and possessions are the poorest of the poor.

I need to be careful that, in the making of my point, I do not offend. I am in touch with many people of means who are quite generous. But I am also aware that a significant majority of affluent people entirely lack a generous spirit.

A South African Afrikaner woman related to me an experience she and a friend had in the past year.

She was black; I was white. We became part of an interracial program in which arrangements were made for us to live with a black family in a township for a week and then to live with a white, rather wealthy family for a week. When we arrived in Alexandria (a township), we were taken to a home that was little more than a shack with two rooms. There were five in the family. The interior of that home was immaculate, even though the family owned next to nothing.

We soon learned that the husband and wife intended to turn over the one bed in the home to us. For a week the entire family slept on the dirt floor in one room while we slept in the bed in the other room. At meal time, we were served first and given the best of what the family had to offer. Everything they had was ours to use.

Then the following week we went to Pretoria to live with a white family. The home was beautiful with several bedrooms. But I was stunned when we were directed to a recreation room and told that we could unroll our sleeping bags on the floor. That week we slept on the floor in a home that had several bedrooms that went unused.

Jesus sat at the temple gate watching wealthy people pour their coins into the temple treasury and, apparently, doing it in such a way that a loud noise—attracting attention—was heard each time. None of these were named; none were pointed out as exemplary of generosity. Who was? "A poor widow came and put in two very small copper coins, worth only a fraction of a penny" (Mark 12:42).

Mark, the storyteller, writes, "Calling his disciples to him . . ." (v. 43). My sense is that the disciples were preoccupied with a score of things worth watching and discussing. And Jesus suddenly called them to join Him. "Hey, I want you watch this," I can hear Him saying. "Watch this woman." He points and says, "There . . . that one!"

Who would watch a woman this poor when there were so many impressive others to watch? But the Son of God seems to be saying, "Watch." And then He says, "I tell you the truth, this poor widow has put more into the treasury than all the others. They all gave out of their wealth; but she, out of her poverty, put in everything—all she had to live on" (vv. 43–44).

Natural eyes seek out glamour and power. The eyes of the Son of God seek out real generosity.

The big picture of the resilient person must include these questions: What can I give out of what I can do? What can I give through what I am? And what can I give through what I have?

I am blessed with special friends who work with these questions and take them quite seriously, in fact, work them out every day of their lives. Perhaps it explains why, when we get together, there is little small talk or energy spent complaining or slandering. We don't dote on the fact that the church is changing its ways without regard to our opinions. We don't waste time running down people who have made bad mistakes. Rather, we fill our conversation with lots of grace. There are plenty of stories to tell that evince laughter, tears, excitement. And this is the way it should be when friends gather—if the big picture of their lives includes generosity.

III

RESILIENT PEOPLE RUN FREE OF THE WEIGHT OF THE PAST

They understand the importance of repairing the past.

They respect the power of memory.

They practice repentance.

They are quick to forgive.

They overflow with gratitude.

They squeeze the past for all its wisdom.

IN LOSING, THERE IS LEARNING

I am at the starting line of an 800-meter run. To my right is a runner I've been thinking about for several weeks. He represents the heavy competition for a league championship in the 800 meters next month. If I can beat him today, it will provide the confidence I will need for the year's biggest race.

The serious preparation for today began a week ago when Marvin Goldberg asked to see me in the classroom where he taught chemistry and physics. When I arrived, I could see a chalked diagram of two 400-meter tracks, each representing a lap of the 800-meter event.

MWG quickly came to the point. "Gordie, it will be difficult for you to beat [he named the man who now stood beside me at the starting line]. If you win, it will be because you have a better running strategy and because you run your fastest 800-meter time. I don't want you to compete with him. I want you to compete with the clock. There are four parts to this race, and I want us to work all week on a running plan for each part." Goldberg moved to the chalkboard.

"I want you to run for time from the very start of the race. *Let him run whatever pace he wants.* You're going to run for time." He began to write numbers on the board, times he wanted me to run for each 200 meters.

———

"Now, here's where I want you to pick up the pace." Again he pointed to a spot on the second diagram. "And at this point"—now he marked a point on the final turn—"you'll want to use everything else you've got left. You're conditioned to carry that pace for the rest of the race. Run those times, and I think the race can be yours. We'll have people on the watch at each 200 meters so you'll know exactly how you're doing."

Each day that week, we practiced the coach's strategy. Most of my workouts corresponded to the exact times planned for each 200 meters. Other runners played the "rabbit," and I got the feel of the places on the track where I was to increase the pace, when I was to back it off, and when I was to "kick."

Now the day we had mapped out so carefully had arrived. The gun sounded, and the runners sprang off the line. But "sprang" is, perhaps, not the correct word, because it was clear within a few seconds that the pack of runners was not off to a fast pace. And neither was the one man I needed to beat. Before we reached the first turn I was telling myself that this race was going to be a laugher. I began to assume that it was mine to win in any way I chose.

We call this *hubris*—a numbing pride that displaces common sense. Instantly, all the training, all the strategy conversations, all the intensity of preparation was forgotten. My concentration was gone.

That's when I remembered the very special girl who had come to see me run. I knew that she was standing at the end of the back stretch just before the second turn. She would be impressed, I thought, if I approached that point well in the lead. So I jumped ahead of the pack of runners and flew down the track toward the girl and the curve. Soon I'd forgotten everyone in the race except myself and how I must look to the spectators . . . and the girl. If any teammate called out the 200-meter time split, I never heard it.

As I rounded the curve, 300 meters into the race, I appeared to be well in command of the race.

At 400 meters, the halfway point, I was still in the lead, but totally out of touch with the running plan developed a week before in the coach's classroom. And that's why at the 600-meter point, the fatigue hit, and as I began to fade, the man I'd thought about for weeks passed me as if I was standing still. Where had he come from? And where were these other runners coming from that suddenly seemed to surround me? That day I finished a dismal third . . . or fourth, maybe fifth.

If there was ever a time when I did not want to face Marvin Goldberg, it was then. I had not run according to any of the strategy we had plotted on the board in the lab; I had ignored all of the training we'd done that week with the help of several teammates.

"If you will trust me . . ." MWG had once said to me when I'd first joined the team. I had violated that trust relationship. And now I had to account for my performance.

"Gordie, come here, please." The tone of the coach's voice underscored that this would not be a happy conversation. "Gordie, why don't you tell me what you had on your mind as you ran?"

Did I dare tell him that this was mostly about a girl? Probably not. I must have found other reasons that made more sense. Quietly, patiently, he reviewed the original plan and then noted the actual time splits I'd run and how they contrasted with the plan.

"Gordie, this race has only one value now. What you might learn from it. I want you to think through every step you took. What made you choose to do what you did? I tell you, my growing fear is that you will walk through life learning most things the hard way. You seem to have to lose in order to learn how to win. Today you didn't trust me; you didn't run the plan; you totally underestimated your competition. On Monday I want you to tell me why."

"I'm sorry, sir," I said. "This is the last thing I will learn the hard way," which, unfortunately, was not true. It was a weekend of difficult reflection.

That was the day I began to understand the front edge of an important principle leading to resilience. Resilient people face the brutal facts of their mistakes, their experiences, their sins, their blessings. And they learn from them. That's how they *repair the past.*

TWELVE

RESILIENT PEOPLE UNDERSTAND THE IMPORTANCE OF REPAIRING THE PAST

———

*"Your sins are forgiven . . . your faith has saved you . . .
go in peace."*
—JESUS, TO A WOMAN OF QUESTIONABLE REPUTE (LUKE 7:48, 50)

Summers are short in New England when compared to summers
to the south of us. So we Yankees take the warm weather seriously,
and we try to use every pleasant day to the greatest possible advantage. We grab quick vacations, organize frequent picnics, and head
for the lake as often as we can.

But we also spend a lot of time making repairs around our
homes. We touch up cracked paint, replace rotting boards, and check
for leaks in the roof. Delay this maintenance work and you will soon
be living with much greater consequences when winter returns. The
task will no longer be *repair*. It may become *reconstruction*.

And the same is true about one's inner life. We carry within ourselves all our yesterdays, the experiences and influences that have happened from our birth (and maybe before) to this present moment. These yesterdays can powerfully affect *today*—the right-now—and dominate our relationships, our choices, our views of ourselves, even our understanding of God. If our yesterdays are in a state of good repair, they provide strength for today. If not repaired, they create havoc.

Resilient people know this. Ask any of them, and they will tell you in language of their own choosing that one cannot live in a spiritually healthy fashion with an unrepaired past.

Jacob, a man found deep in the Old Testament, lived large parts of his life with an unrepaired past. He was the one, you may remember, who took advantage of his brother, Esau, and manipulated him out of his rights of inheritance. Then when things got hot between them, he fled the country. When it came time to return home, he did so with dread, fearing the worst in retribution from Esau. Lots and lots of worry and fear because he didn't take the principle of a repaired past seriously.

Repairing the past is best done immediately; someone should have told that to Jacob. Patching relationships that are wounded; dealing with regrets that fester in the soul; letting go of negative feelings toward someone who has betrayed a relationship. Neglect this and one's life deteriorates.

As long as these matters go unrepaired, they usually become destructive. Sometimes they lie deep within us as if asleep, almost forgotten. Then they are awakened at some strange, unexpected moment, and they affect our thinking and our choices. These unrepaired issues will mark a marriage relationship, work habits, our sense of ourselves, even our understanding of God. In short, an unrepaired past doesn't go away. It remains and speaks up and into the present of our life-journeys.

———

I am once again in South Africa and have spoken at a conference for pastors and Christian leaders. After giving a talk, I invite people in the audience to come to the front of the room and kneel if they seek a blessing of some kind. An African pastor steps forward, but while others kneel, he comes directly to me and buries his face in my neck and begins to sob. Heavy sobs.

When he can compose himself, he says in a raspy whisper, "I hate the white man; I hate the white man, and I can't get rid of the hate. I need a blessing that will help me get rid of this hate. It's destroying me."

In a later conversation he relates a moment in the days of apartheid when he was only twelve years of age. On a journey with his family, he'd needed a bathroom and searched for one that was not restricted to "whites only." When he saw a men's room in a gas station, he went in. A moment later, as he stood at the urinal, an enormous white man came through the door and shouted, "What are you doing in here?"

Terrified, all he could say was, "The sign said, 'Men.'"

"You're not a man; you're an animal," the white man screamed. And he picked the boy up (before he was finished urinating) and literally tossed him out the door.

"I have hated and feared white men ever since," he says to me. "Even these pastors. I worship with them; I work with them; I go to their conferences. But I have hatred in my heart for them. And it began back there at that gas station."

I think of this pastor every time I launch into the subject of a repaired past. If ever a man sought such repair, I think it was him. An unrepaired past, filled with resentment, was killing his spirit, and he was prepared to do anything that would heal a long-wounded heart.

I am not an educated psychologist. But I think I've learned

much from those who are. And I hear them constantly calling attention to a person's *past*, making it abundantly clear that an unsettled past can have a powerfully negative effect upon a person's ability to sustain a vigorous life.

But long before psychologists were saying what we probably all discern in these twenty-first-century times, the Bible was dealing with the issue of unrepaired past, though it didn't use psychological vocabulary to make the point. Most of the time the Bible just offers stories, and the implications become obvious to the serious reader.

Take, for example, the Genesis story of Joseph. Born into a family of a dozen brothers, he became the target of severe familial rivalry. I've always thought that Joseph was unwise when he flouted his dreams before his brothers, but maybe I don't understand the entire story. Anyway, the brothers despised him. Perhaps they had an uneasy feeling that, because he had his father's special favor, he would end up as king of the hill in the future.

The brothers waited for the opportune moment when they could rid themselves of him. When that moment came, they pounced and would have killed Joseph on the spot had Reuben, the firstborn, not intervened and convinced them to hold off for a while. But shortly thereafter, when Reuben was "away from his desk," the rest of the brothers sold Joseph to an Egypt-bound caravan and assumed that he was out of their lives forever.

Talk about resilience! While this awful set of circumstances would have destroyed the spirits of most people, Joseph seemed to adapt marvelously when he arrived in Egypt. Sold to Potiphar, a military type, he launched into the rest of his life as a slave . . . but, apparently, a very, very good one. Soon he was chief of slaves, executive vice president, we might say, of all of Potiphar's estate. The whole "store" was in his hands. It is a great tribute to the power of Joseph's integrity and trust in God's purposes for his life.

The tension in the story comes from Potiphar's wife, who ultimately accused him of attempted assault and, out of her own rage, assured that Joseph would land in prison.

Resilience again! Soon Joseph was running the jail (this is a great story). And it is out of that incongruous set of circumstances—specifically, that the jail put him in proximity to the Egyptian pharaoh—that he came to the attention of national leadership. A few dream interpretations later, everything changed. *And soon the man was running the country.*

Then came the issue of Joseph's past and the test as to whether it was in a state of repair. Enter his brothers, who came to Egypt in search of food when a severe famine hit Canaan. When they arrived, they hadn't a clue as to who it was that had the key to the storehouse.

It seemed at times as if Joseph was playing mind games with his brothers. He knew who they were, but they had not yet figured out who he was. In quiet moments there were several times when Joseph abandoned his official posture and, in hiding, wept great tears of sadness.

We don't need a psychologist to tell us what is going on here. We can feel it—especially those of us who have felt the awesome pain of family dysfunction in our pasts. We've wept those tears.

Look at the brothers. Even before they recognized Joseph, they smelled something wrong. The guilt and remorse of the violence of the past was not far below the surface of their lives. It took just one little inconvenience during this Egyptian trip for their confidence to be shaken. When Joseph put their backs to the wall, they disintegrated. The first thing that came to their minds? The memory of selling Joseph to the Ishmaelite caravan.

> "Surely we are being punished because of our brother. We saw how distressed he was when he pleaded with us for his life, but we would not listen; that's why this distress has come upon us." (Gen. 42:21)

Why would these men equate a present hassle with something that had occurred more than a dozen years ago?

The only possible answer is that each of them had carried this unsettled memory in his heart all of these years. All it took was a bad moment to trigger it, bring it to the surface, and cause a connection to be made.

Reuben, the only brother who had spoken up for Joseph, tried to put distance between himself and his brothers: "Didn't I tell you not to sin against the boy? But you wouldn't listen! Now we must give an accounting for his blood" (v. 22).

This dance between Joseph and his brothers finally reached a moment of disclosure.

> Then Joseph could no longer control himself before all his attendants, and he cried out, "Have everyone leave my presence!" So there was no one with Joseph when he made himself known to his brothers. And he wept so loudly that the Egyptians heard him, and Pharaoh's household heard about it. Joseph said to his brothers, "I am Joseph! Is my father still living?" (45:1–3)

The pathos of this moment must have been astounding. We are watching a man bring his past to closure, first in his interior life and now in the key relationships that had been broken so many years ago.

But the brothers? As I said, another story.

> His brothers were not able to answer him, because they were terrified at his presence. (45:3)

Unlike Joseph, who was spiritually weightless in terms of any anger or resentment, the full weight of the brothers' past hung on them. One can only imagine the guilt and the paralyzing fear in their hearts. The past—unrepaired—now informed the present. And the message wasn't pretty.

Joseph could easily have fallen into this web of a broken-down, unrepaired past, and the consequences would have been unspeakable. First, he would never have ascended to the level of biblical character that marks him as one of the great champions of the Bible. Second, he would never have come to a place where he would be in a position to save lives by the thousands. And third, he would never, ever have been able to build a bridge back to his family . . . to his father . . . to his roots.

Joseph's father, Jacob, died. And the brothers—still not in a complete state of repair—resurrected their fears that Joseph might yet seek vengeance. "What if," they asked, "Joseph holds a grudge against us and pays us back for all the wrongs we did to him?" (Gen. 50:15).

Joseph's response:

"Don't be afraid. Am I in the place of God? You intended to harm me, *but God intended it for good to accomplish what is now being done, the saving of many lives.* So then, don't be afraid. I will provide for you and your children." And he reassured them and spoke kindly to them. (vv. 19–21, emphasis mine)

That last sentence! "He reassured them and spoke kindly to them." Those are indeed the actions of a man whose past is repaired. This is a primary quality of a resilient person.

In a speech on the moral authority of U.S. presidents, historian David Abshire said, "How many of our presidents in recent times have had personal crises because they never put away childish things, never grew out of their hang-ups, never learned from mistakes, never quite put the nation ahead of themselves?"[1]

The words (perhaps reflecting those of the apostle Paul) "putting away childish things" grabbed my attention, because they speak to my point. Resilient people put away childish things. And that's what Joseph did.

As I said, summers tend to be short in New England. So we use the time well to repair our homes and other things that will face the abuse of winter. So it is with the soul. It must be in a constant state of repair—if you are to be a resilient person.

THIRTEEN

RESILIENT PEOPLE RESPECT THE POWER OF MEMORY

I may have been five years old on the day my mother sent me off on my first shopping experience. Her instructions were clear. Cross Braddock Avenue—while she watched, of course—go to the meat store on the other side, and give the butcher an envelope that contained the order (for bologna) and the money. It was an exciting moment for any child wanting to demonstrate that he was growing up.

I did as I was told, and everything went smoothly until the butcher handed me the bologna in a bag and said, "You've got two cents change coming."

I have no idea why I said it, but I told him, "Keep the change." Somewhere I'd heard this phrase and must have thought it appropriate for the moment.

I still recall the butcher's surprise at my precocious manner. "Oh, no," he said; he couldn't keep the change. Never! And he put the two pennies into the envelope I'd brought and insisted that I give them to my mother.

A moment later I recrossed the street and gave my waiting

mother her bologna and the change. Then I ran off to resume my play. But soon my mother's voice summoned me to the house.

The butcher had called our home (Fieldstone 4185) and related the "keep-the-change" episode to my mother. In our neighborhood, people did this sort of thing.

It was clear that my mother didn't think that what I'd done was cute. "You *always* bring every penny home," she said. "Your father works hard for every penny. You *never* say, 'Keep the change.'"

Now comes the sillier part of this story. For sixty years I have always—always!—waited patiently at any store counter for the change . . . even if the change is but a penny. There must be times when some clerk wonders why I would wait for such a small amount of money, but there's a voice inside me—Mother's voice—that says, "You bring every penny home." I may leave good tips when appropriate, but I can't ever bring myself to say, "Keep the change."

This is all about the power and reach of memory. I am sympathetic with the idea that our impressions of every event in our lives are stored in these incredible memories of ours. And when we least expect it, these memories influence how we live life in the present.

Resilient people believe this, and that is why they are careful to keep memories in a state of good repair—as Joseph did—lest unhealthy ones gain control of today's attitudes and behaviors.

It is said that half of what we will learn in a lifetime is learned before the age of five. How one arrives at this conclusion is unknown to me, but it makes sense. And it also provides the groundwork for an idea that has stuck with me for some time:

> A significant part of who we are, what we do, and how we relate to others is shaped by our impressions of the experiences of the first ten years of our lives.

If this is even half-true, it becomes a monumental idea to deal with. It suggests that some of the major building blocks of how we see life and handle it were all put into place in those first years. What if some of those blocks were the wrong ones, or what if they were put into place in the wrong way?

When I asked a ninety-three-year-old man if he and his ninety-year-old wife ever have conflict, he assured me that they do. I asked him how they treat each other in such moments, and he told me how important it is that he speak tenderly to her. When I asked why, he told me that when his wife was a girl, her father always spoke to her in a harsh and hurtful tone of voice. "Whenever she hears any man speak in an angry manner, the feelings of hurt and fear return."

"But that was eighty to eighty-five years ago," I said, speaking of her father. "Are you telling me that she still remembers—"

"More than ever!" he responded emphatically.

In our earliest years we explore our feelings and emotions. We watch those who are "largest" in our lives and note how and when they express anger, joy, sadness, or fear. And we take our cues from what we see.

We learn how to give and receive love in the first ten years of life. The ways in which we feel the affection and tenderness of a parent (the way we observe our parents loving one another) become a model of our understanding how to love others as we grow older.

Most of us will learn our basic communication skills in those first years—how to talk, how to listen. We will gain or lose the confidence of expressing our thoughts and concepts to others. And if that confidence is not gained, we may spend the rest of our lives reluctant to engage with others in easygoing discourse. We will retreat, withdraw, and let others do the talking, speak only when spoken to, or feel pressure when someone challenges us to speak our minds.

I suspect we form our basic work habits in those earliest years. Will work be a challenge, or something to be avoided? Will it be done with excellence and thoroughness, or done poorly? Will it often be finished, or left incomplete?

What about the possibility that our basic view of God is probably fashioned in the first ten years?

My earliest impression of God, for example, was that He rained on parades. Which is to say that, for me, the God of the Bible was hardly the patron of fun.

My childhood impression was that life was full of disappointments and that God liked it this way. From that I cultivated the notion that God probably did not want me to have a new bike, be selected first for the pickup baseball games at the corner lot, or enjoy the favor of the teacher in first grade.

I realize now that this unfortunate view of God permeated my teen years and my young adulthood. And there came a moment when I had to rewrite the script and renounce the earlier impressions written upon my soul. An example, of course, of what it means to repair the past.

I have always suspected that this deficient perception of God was a problem for David the psalmist. His family doesn't seem to have been a secure place for him. What's to be said about a father who trotted out all of his sons, except David, when Samuel the prophet came seeking a candidate for Israel's next king? When Samuel reviewed them all and received a thumbs-down signal from God, he asked Jesse the father, "Is this all?" And the answer came back, "We've got the runt of the family out in the fields, but I didn't think he was worth bringing in." (This, incidentally, is my own translation of the story).

I ask myself how I would have felt if I'd been out in the fields and knew that my father didn't consider me valuable enough to number me among his sons. And would that have carried beyond my view of my father to my view of God Himself?

My bet is that David carried this memory throughout his life, and it drove him to find in God a substitute father. Which isn't really a bad idea at all. Read these words and see if they do not express a lifelong broken heart of a son who never felt valued with his earthly father.

> Hear my voice when I call, O LORD, be merciful to me and answer me. My heart says of you, "Seek his face!" Your face, LORD, I will seek. Do not hide your face from me, do not turn your servant away in anger; you have been my helper. Do not reject me or forsake me, O God my Savior. Though my father and mother forsake me, the LORD will receive me. (Ps. 27:7–10)

I see David repairing his past with such words. Rather than deny the sadness or the wounds of the past, he puts the truth on the table and deals with it. To be sure, there were other dimensions of his past that he apparently ignored. But here he does commendable work.

Resilient people treat their pasts and the stories therein seriously. And when they perceive connections between the past and the present, they ask God for the power, the insight, and the appropriate process to deal with them. If necessary, they repair things.

Each time I hold a penny in my hand, a sixty-year memory of a butcher shop is enlivened. Keep the penny? Yeah! My mother once said it was important, and the memory influences me.

———

Many years ago I was speaking at a conference, and at the end of a session a woman approached me. Introducing herself, she said, "I was your babysitter when you were a child."

We visited for a while, and I found myself enthralled with this touch from my past.

I remember this conversation as one of the first times that I became intensely curious about what I was like as a child. What had been the things that formed me? I knew she had some answers.

When our conversation ended, I asked a favor. "Would you be willing to write me a long letter and attempt to recall everything you remember about me as a child?" She said she would be delighted, and we parted company.

Several weeks later, the letter I'd requested arrived. Today it lies somewhere in one of our many family scrapbooks, a treasure that I shall reread in my old, old years. The letter was several pages long, single-spaced, very detailed. It was written by one with a sharp memory.

This was the letter that prompted me to begin to arrange my memories—to begin putting them in order and to see what significance could be gained from them. It began to dawn on me that my memories are a large part of who I am, and if my memories are untidy, in disarray . . . if they are filled with unresolved issues (as in the case of the brothers of Joseph), then my resilience is diminished.

In the letter my former babysitter recalled that my favorite form of play as a four-year-old was to take her to the church—my father's church—next to our home. We would enter the empty sanctuary together, and I would usher her to a particular seat. And then I would walk on to the pulpit just as I saw my father do it each week.

I would kneel at the seat where he knelt each week. And then, after an appropriate pause for prayer, I would go to the pulpit, open the hymn book, and announce a song. And we—I, the pastor; my babysitter, the church attendee—would make our way through a worship service: songs, a prayer, an offering, announcements, and a sermon. Then I would offer a benediction—my hand upraised in blessing as I'd often seen my father's upraised—and then I would go to the back door and prepare to shake her hand when she left the sanctuary. Any wonder that I have spent most of my life as a pastor?

In the attempt to arrange my memories, I found that most of them fall under one of three categories:

1. They are about the key people who have influenced me, for good or ill.

2. They are about the major ideas that have guided me, noble or ignoble.

3. They are about the critical events that have changed me, happy or sad.

On those occasions when I have engaged in what is sometimes called *executive coaching*, I have used these three categories to help people sort out the pathways of their lives.

First I ask them to partition their lives into five-year blocks (0–5, 5–10, 10–15, etc.). Then I invite them to do their best to fill each block with the names of *the influential people, the great ideas and the critical events* that relate to each block. I warn that this cannot be done in an evening or a weekend. It will likely take several weeks if not months. The recapture of one memory often leads to another. We become surprised and sometimes shocked at what lurks deep within that has been stored for years and years.

I suggest remembering the homes in which one lived, names of best friends, schoolteachers, and neighbors. Once we begin to identify these "landmarks" of life, the memories begin to flow.

I think God had something like this in mind when He led Israel out of Egypt and across the wilderness toward the promised land. From the very start, God freshened their memories as a people. At the earlier moments of the journey, He taught them the ceremony of the Passover.

"This is a day you are to commemorate; for the generations to come you shall celebrate it as a festival to the LORD—*a lasting ordinance*." (Ex. 12:14, emphasis mine)

Throughout the journey, which lasted for forty years, God gave names to places of significance. He had Israel construct altars and monuments here and there. Remember the crossing of the Jordan into the promised land?

The LORD said to Joshua, "Choose twelve men from among the people, one from each tribe, and tell them to take up twelve stones from the middle of the Jordan from right where the priests stood and to carry them over with you and put them down at the place where you stay tonight." (Josh. 4:1–3)

Later Joshua would speak of this exercise:

"[These stones will] serve as a sign among you. In the future, when your children ask you, 'What do these stones mean?' tell them that the flow of the Jordan was cut off before the ark of the covenant of the LORD . . . These stones are to be a memorial to the people of Israel forever." (vv. 6–7)

In other words: remembering is important. Remembering correctly is important. Remembering appreciatively is important.

———

When I work through the five-year blocks of my life, my grandmother takes an important place in my list of influential people. She seemed to love me fiercely. If I had not given my life to God, I think she would have done it for me.

Grandmother was the first serious pray-er in my life. Since my grandfather was a missionary leader with his face pointed toward Europe, Grandma insisted that I learn the map of Europe—its rivers, its great cities, its people groups, and its rich history. She unashamedly bribed me to memorize all the European nations, promising two brand-new dollar bills (no small amount of money then) when I could repeat their names with no mistakes. Memorizing Ephesians 6 was worth a pencil sharpener—something I'd long coveted.

There are many other key persons I could place in the five-year blocks of life. Not all of them were particularly good people. There are those who are remembered because they brought pain, hurt, or humiliation. These have to be included among the key people also. And when we meet someone in our adult years that reminds us of them, we struggle with strange feelings of dislike or fear or anger. And that's one of those times when repairing the past becomes so significant.

———

In the arranging of memories, it is important to trace the major ideas that have guided one's life throughout the years. Have the ideas changed? Which have turned out to be false or misguiding?

A prevailing idea that hung on my life for many years was one I call the "destiny" idea. There is something very important you are to do in your life. You cannot miss it. You must find out what it is and go toward it. Don't be like Jonah, who tried to run from his destiny. You don't want to end up in the belly of some whale. Think destiny. As one cartoon character once reflected, "It's a difficult thing to live with a destiny hanging around your neck."

There were, of course, the unique ideas that prevailed if one grew up in an observant Christian environment. You must make sure all your friends have heard about Jesus (I wasn't good at this); you don't want any of them going to hell because you didn't tell them the gospel

(I certainly didn't, but somehow this was not a helpful motivation). You must determine whether or not you have been called into the ministry, because you will live in judgment all of your life if you had a call and didn't obey it (I worried long and hard about this one).

These ideas shaped the first ten years of my life. For good or for ill. And there were some of them I had to reappraise in later years. They could be the sources of unnecessary guilt or they could be misguiding ideas about the true nature of the God of the Bible.

———

Another question in the arrangement of memories has to do with critical events. These are those unique events that change us forever. They stand out from the routines of every day; they surprise us; they are never forgotten.

James MacGregor Burns in his classic book on leadership writes:

Sigmund Freud, before going to sleep one evening when he was seven or eight years old . . . [from this point on it is Freud who is writing] "disregarded the rules which modesty lays down and obeyed the calls of nature in my parents' bedroom while they were present. In the course of his reprimand, my father let fall the words: 'The boy will come to nothing.' This must have been a frightful blow (an insult) to my ambition, for references to this scene are still constantly recurring in my dreams and are always linked with an enumeration of my achievements and successes, as though I wanted to say: 'You see, I have come to something.'"[1]

This, I think, would rank in Freud's life as a critical event. Although seemingly insignificant at the moment—a (perhaps) frightened little boy wetting his pants—the event turns out to be a life changer, a touch point that will contribute to the shaping of his whole future. And, I might add, a tiny event that changed not only Freud's life, but, you could say, world history.

The question which arises from the pile of our memories is this: What do I do with them? What are the chief responses to a past so full of things that, if one is not careful, can weigh us down and make the long race of life a difficult journey? The Biblical people had at least four answers to this question. The way of repentance, the discipline of forgiveness, the life of gratitude, and the search for wisdom. Each has explosive implications for repairing the past when fully understood.

FOURTEEN

RESILIENT PEOPLE PRACTICE REPENTANCE

About 350 years ago, an English preacher, John Bunyan, wrote *Pilgrim's Progress*, an allegorical description of the Christian life. Written while he spent time in jail for his convictions, Bunyan described the journey of Pilgrim, or Christian, who left his home in the City of Destruction and headed for the Celestial City. Along the way he met one character after another . . . some good, some bad.

No picture in this vivid book impresses me more than one of the earliest, that of Christian carrying a huge burden on his back. Soon it becomes clear that the burden is the accumulation of his sins—the issues of his past.

At one point early in his journey, Christian runs into Mr. Pliable. Pliable is the kind of man we call a *pleaser*, one who wants to make everybody happy, who is easily convinced, and who will stick with something as long as the way is easy and uncomplicated. He is usually optimistic, even enthusiastic.

Pliable finds it difficult to understand why Christian can't move faster as they travel . . . perhaps even run a bit.

"I can't run," Christian says to him. "This burden on my back is simply too heavy."

Pliable is uncomprehending. He has no similar burden, because he resists looking back to see what's there, what his past is all about. So Pliable just lives from moment to moment, and he is oblivious to the fact that his inner world has filled up with all sorts of stuff. As long as he can ignore it, he's OK . . . for the moment.

When the two—Christian and Pliable—fall into a swamp (Bunyan calls it the Swamp of Despair) into which all the sewage of the surrounding towns drains, Pliable is quick to want to quit the journey. He wants out; he wants to head back to where he came from. And the two men split. Pliable is last seen running back to where he came from. But Christian—still loaded down with his burden—presses forward toward the place where, he has been told, his burden will be lifted from his back.

For Bunyan's Christian, everything is about dealing with or repairing the past—getting that burden off of his back. He would fully understand the biblical writer's challenge to "throw off everything that hinders and the sin that so easily entangles" (Heb. 12:1).

It appears to me that there are three ways people set out to repair the past.

The first is to blow it off, live only in the present and, perhaps, the future. We call this denial. In effect, the past does not exist for any practical purpose. Don't think about it; don't ask what damage lies back there; don't ask if there is mopping up to do. I have met people who live this way, and it seems to me that Pliable adopted this strategy.

I am thinking of a man who found the issues of the past too difficult to deal with. There were too many damaged relationships, too many regrets. His solution? Simply walk away from the past, tell the people you've known all your life that you're no longer interested in any connection with them at all. Letters will go unread; phone calls will not be accepted; holiday greetings will be ignored. This amounts to creating a whole new life for oneself. Bottom line: my burden ceases to be a burden because I won't recognize its existence. Admittedly, this way can work for a while.

While the man I've just mentioned has adopted a rather dramatic strategy, there are many others who simply bury yesterday in a flood of distracting experiences. In other words, they outrun the past. Acquire new things, new relationships, new jobs, new activities. Just keep on running. Perhaps, they reason, the past will not have time to catch up.

A second option for dealing with the past is to accept the burden and get used to it. This means living with its increasing weight, recognizing the fact that life will get slower and slower as the burden gets greater and greater. It seems to me that Saul, king of Israel, falls into this category. Rather than deal with his own shortcomings, his burden, he became obsessed with the young David and chased him all over the wilderness with a mind to kill him. If only he had been willing to face himself and his own burden. But it seemed simpler to carry it and obsess about David.

One time at a conference, a man talked with me off in a corner. He was aware of things I've written concerning the interior life. As we talked, I could sense that there was a deep secret—a knot—in his life. When I challenged him on the matter, he acknowledged that I was correct. There was a *burden*. But as much as he wanted to, he couldn't even bring himself to put it into words. But it must have been serious, because he admitted he would lose his family, his status as a Christian leader, and his job if the secret was ever disclosed.

"How long have you been living with this?" I asked.

"Oh, at least twenty years," he replied.

"And what are you doing about it?"

"I just have to live with it. I have to face it every day of my life and wonder when, if ever, it's going to come out."

My bet is that we're talking about a lot of people like this man.

They have mindlessly concluded that their burden is part of the cost of living. They'll do what they can under the circumstances. But the burden of the past will always be factored into their journey.

Which leads me to the third way that the past can be managed. *Repair it!* This is a most favorable option and made possible by the grace given to us in Jesus Christ and His death on the cross.

Repairing the past begins with repentance. The word is associated with the Greek word *metanoia,* which the Greeks used to describe actions like remorse, changing one's mind, and altering one's direction.

Repentance was not always a religious word. The word comes out of an ancient world where travelers had few roads, no signs, no lights, and no maps. Getting lost was common. This meant that the moment a traveler became uneasy as to where he was, he had to stop and say, "I'm lost." That was followed by a search for the right way and then a retracing of steps until he was back on the right path.

In the Bible, words like *sin* (meaning "missing the mark"), *lost, seek, repent, saved* (or rescued), and *found* are all part of the vocabulary of repairing the past. They describe the process by which a redeeming God, who always has an ear open for a repentant person, reaches out in love and removes the burden one has been carrying for so long.

In a description of the act of repentance, Jesus told the story of the prodigal son, a young man who had squandered at least half of his father's wealth before making a total mess of his own life. When he reached a point at which swine were eating better than he was, he finally acknowledged that he was lost.

> "How many of my father's hired men have food to spare, and here I am starving to death! I will set out and go back to my father and say to him: 'Father, I have sinned against heaven and against you.'" (Luke 15:17–18)

These are the words of one who is saying, "I'm lost!" *I have sinned* (missed the mark) says it all.

I don't think there are many books with my name on them that don't get to this subject of repentance sooner or later. Reason: I had to go deep into the subject in my own life-journey. Not as a student of repentance, but as a practitioner. I know the heart of the prodigal quite well.

As I write these paragraphs, I am looking out the window of my study onto a small grassy meadow. It is part of the place we have called *Peace Ledge,* where we have had a home for twenty-five years. At one edge of this meadow is a lovely garden, one of three which Gail tends throughout the New England summer. Right now it is brilliant with the colors of flowers.

Twenty-five years ago this wasn't a meadow, nor was there a garden with flowers. It was an overgrown field with every kind of wild vegetation. Strewn across the ground were rocks and boulders of various kinds. Around the edge of the field were (and still are) stone walls, which indicate that farmers of previous generations were forever digging up boulders and rocks and piling them along the edge. Thus the walls.

When we bought the land we call Peace Ledge, we determined to turn this field into a meadow. That meant cutting the vegetation so that the grasses would be free to grow. And it meant ridding the field of most of those rocks and boulders. That was no small task.

First we removed the large stones (bigger than a breadbasket). Then we went for the smaller boulders and rocks (basketball size). Finally, we went back a third time and combed the field—now becoming a meadow—for rocks of small size that would wreak havoc on the rotating blade of a tractor mower. It took at least two years to do this.

I liken this effort to the initial exercise of repentance, a spiritual exercise. Just as one grooms a field by ridding it of its rocks and boulders, so one grooms the interior life and identifies the events and attitudes of the past that have offended God and the people of one's community. One names them and acknowledges responsibility for them. This is important. One does not deal in excuses or explanations. One simply accepts responsibility and asks, "What can be done to make this right?"

As a child, I called this being sorry for my sins. As an adult, the language became more sophisticated. But it really wasn't very different. The problem is that, as we get older, we become weary of being sorry for our sins. We become "smarter," and we develop all sorts of ways that help us not have to be so sorry. We create rationales that lessen our responsibility. We blame others, blame the system, blame mitigating circumstances. Anything that helps us not feel so badly about ourselves.

The problem is that while the rationale grows more sophisticated, the burden gets heavier.

Repentance never really was a hot topic for me until my life ran into complete failure twenty years ago. In a moment I shall regret until the day I die, I broke the vows of a very blessed marriage. Call it unfaithfulness; call it infidelity. Call it any name you wish, but it was an event for which there was no explanation or excuse. Today, that episode is so painful to me that I say to myself, *I don't even know (or want to know) the man who did that. Who was he?*

I am sorry to say that it took a failure like that to arouse me to much deeper truths about myself than I would ever have been willing to face under other circumstances.

Like the meadow I see from my study window, my life had seemed free and clear of most large rocks and boulders. When I looked closely and saw the small stones and pebbles in my life, I would cover them with occasional and superficial acknowledgments of my need for grace and forgiveness. But it was all rather routine. After all, I wasn't into pornography; I wasn't abusive with our children; I wasn't embezzling money from the church; and I wasn't attracted to members of the opposite gender (except my wife). In truth, I was a reasonably vanilla man, with some weaknesses and blind spots but no massive sin activities.

And then I made a series of simple, seemingly innocent choices that led to an evil one.

Let me take the story of the meadow one step further. When we cleared the field of its rocks and boulders and cut back the vegetation so that the grasses could grow, we didn't anticipate one thing that the locals could have told us if we'd asked. We didn't know that underneath the soil (shallow as it is) were countless other rocks and boulders, each of which would make their individual appearance in time. As the winter frost went deep into the ground each year, it would thrust up many of these rocks and boulders. In the spring I would climb on my tractor mower and suddenly hear the blade hit a rock I'd never seen before. When I checked, I would be surprised to see the face of a rock peeking up from the soil. I hadn't known it was there before. And when I tried to pry the rock loose, I often discovered that it wasn't a rock; it was a boulder—much bigger than a breadbasket . . . and *it had been there all the time, hidden until now.*

That was my problem. There were rocks—no, *boulders*—hidden deep in the interior parts that I'd not known about. And they needed to be recognized, named, dealt with.

And that's where my colossal failure of twenty years ago brought me. To the recognition that *repentance* is more than being sorry for my sins. It is, first and foremost, a solemn recognition that deep within me lie *rocks,* perhaps unseen right now but capable of appearing at any moment, and they will need the covering grace of God.

Twenty years ago I could not deal with the failure in my life by saying a simple good-night prayer, "Lord, I'm sorry for my sins." I had to face things deep within myself that had produced inexcusable conduct. I had to face squarely the fact that I had hurt the people closest to me. I had broken trusts that had been built over many years. I had threatened a carefully built network of relationships that were life-giving. And I haven't even started to mention what it meant to offend God so grievously.

This is the repentance event: facing what has been done and acknowledging the pain one has caused to others. And doing so without excuse.

Having had to make things right with God, with my wife, and with my family, I then had to stand before fifteen hundred friends who now knew my worst secret and account to them. Today it is hard to believe that Gail and I walked through all of that. But we did, and it has made all the difference in our lives.

Suffice it to say, I understand repentance. It gave me my life back.

Repentance is indispensable to the resilient life. It becomes a habitual spiritual pattern to be practiced regularly. And when a person faces God with an open heart, nothing held back, and when that person relies solely upon the love and grace of Jesus, there is a lightening of the load. The burden is lifted.

Watch the resilient person closely. To use Isaiah's words, "[They] will run and not grow weary, they will walk and not be faint" (40:31). This is the way of the resilient person who has lightened the load through the regular discipline of repentance.

FIFTEEN

RESILIENT PEOPLE ARE QUICK TO FORGIVE

In one of his books, John Claypool related the story of twin brothers who were inseparable. Growing up, they attended the same schools, wore similar clothes, engaged in the same activities. When they reached manhood, they took over the family business—a store—and worked so well together that they were the envy of every businessperson in their community.

One morning, Claypool writes, a customer entered the store and purchased an item for a dollar (this is an old story). The brother who waited on him took the bill, placed it on top of the cash register, and walked to the front of the store with the customer to say good-bye. A while later he returned to the cash register and noted that the dollar was missing. When he asked his brother if he had put the bill in the register, he said he'd never seen it.

"That's funny," the first brother said. "I distinctly remember placing the bill here on the register, and no one else has been in the store since then."

"Had the matter been dropped at that point," Claypool comments, "nothing would have come of the [incident]."

However, an hour later, this time with a noticeable hint of suspicion in his voice, the brother asked again, "Are you sure you didn't see that dollar bill and put it into the register?" The other brother was quick to catch the note of accusation, and flared back in defensive anger.

The incident was the beginning "of the first serious breach of trust that had ever come between these two. It grew wider and wider."

No amount of discussion resolved the issue, and finally the matter crescendoed in an angry decision to dissolve the partnership. A wall was erected dividing the building in two, and what was once a thriving business became two struggling, competitive stores, "each brother trying to enlist allies for himself against the other." Then Claypool added, "This open warfare went on for over twenty years."

Then one day a car with an out-of-state license drove up in front of the stores. A well-dressed man got out and went into one of the sides and inquired how long the merchant had been in business in that location. When he found that it was over twenty years, the stranger said, "Then you are the one with whom I must settle an old score."

The visitor then related an incident from twenty years back. He had been a drifter, he said, moving from town to town, no money, almost nothing to eat.

As I was walking down the alley behind your store, I looked in and saw a dollar bill on top of the cash register. Everyone else was in front of the store. I had been raised in a Christian home and I had never before in all my life stolen anything, but that morning I was so hungry I gave in to the temptation, slipped through the door and took that dollar bill. That act has weighed on my conscience ever since, and I finally decided that I would never be at peace until I came back and faced up to that old sin and made amends. Would you let me now replace that money and pay you whatever is appropriate for damages?

Claypool describes how the storekeeper, now an aging man, began to shake his head in consternation and weep. After a few minutes, when he had gained control of himself, he said to the stranger, "I want you to go next door and repeat the same story you have just told me."

The stranger did it, only this time there were two old men who looked remarkably alike, both weeping uncontrollably.[1]

I don't know whether or not this is a true story. But I must tell you, I cannot read it—and I have read it often—without a bit of emotion of my own. It stirs within me thoughts of relationships of which I have been a part where there was strain (to say the least) or schism (to say the worst).

This is a story about forgiveness, or, rather, the lack of it.

In the years of my life, when I lacked maturity and wisdom, there were times when I found myself in relationships that could not, or so it seemed, be resolved. I was capable of carrying a grudge, of feeling vindictive and wanting to hurt back, of (so typical of me) avoiding an encounter in which a matter might be talked out and brought to an honorable conclusion. Left to myself, I was basically clumsy when it came to conflict and its resolution.

Once I actually think I hated a person for a brief while. If there was a moment of insight when I began to see this dangerous trait for what it was, it came on an airplane as I traveled toward a church where I was to preach for a weekend. I was a young man, and there were feelings boiling inside of me that were frightening. Here I was filled with feelings of resentment toward a colleague. How, I wondered, could I enter any kind of pulpit that weekend and preach the peace of Christ and the grace of God? Even in my immaturity, I knew I couldn't.

I am always reticent to suggest that God has spoken to me. While I believe in the mysterious promptings of God's Holy Spirit, I am uncomfortable in using the kind of language that insinuates a direct conversation. But that day, on that plane, God spoke to me . . . little, hateful me.

Here I was, crying out to God for relief from my hostile feelings (feelings which, years later, I believe were disproportionate and probably unwarranted), and I heard God whisper into my life, *How about forgiveness?* Something simple like that. Three words. That's all I heard. He was asking me to *try forgiveness?* And I decided to try.

The next hour of flying time included one of my life's most memorable spiritual experiences. In an unusual experience of divine encounter, I felt the extraordinary power of God's Spirit empty me of hateful thought. And when the time ended, I felt as if I weighed fifty pounds less.

I have wondered what is behind Simon Peter's question to Jesus in Matthew 18:21, "How many times shall I forgive my brother when he sins against me?" Was he going through my experience? Was this a discussion driven by someone in Peter's life who was a constant irritant? A fellow fisherman? One of the other disciples? His mother-in-law?

It's clear that Peter thought he was being rather magnanimous by suggesting that seven repetitions of forgiveness were a fairly noble gesture. What shock there must have been, therefore, when Jesus upped the ante, saying, "I tell you, not seven times, but seventy-seven times" (v. 22). The Lord might as well have said, "You never stop forgiving."

In the maturing years of my life, I learned much about forgiveness. Forgiveness, I came to see, is about cleaning up the memory by renouncing and flushing vengeful feelings about other people. Forgiveness is about surrendering the right for vengeance and retribution. It is about acknowledging that we are all failures in one way or another and that we stand on level ground with any offender before the cross, where God, in Christ, forgave us. None of us has a claim to superiority over any other in God's presence. Forgiveness is, in part, facing that hard reality.

Paul, writing to the Ephesians, was aware that most of his readers were fresh out of pagan lifestyles where forgiveness was a foreign word. They had been raised in an environment that applauded vengeance. Thus he wrote to them: "Be kind and compassionate to one another, *forgiving* each other, just as in Christ God forgave you" (Eph. 4:32, emphasis mine).

If a person has ever been forgiven for something awful that he has done—and I have been—he knows what being the recipient of forgiveness is all about. He learns that forgiveness is not a single-shot event. *It is a process.* Someone has been hurt, offended, betrayed, but has chosen not to seek punishment.

There is a deep part of us that does not want to forgive. Vengeance is our default reaction to offense. We want another to hurt even as we have been hurt. Thus forgiveness is foreign to the human condition. It has to be learned; it comes with discipline. It is a proactive choice: I will not demand retribution; I will choose to live and think *as if nothing happened.*

The past cannot be repaired without the practice of forgiveness, renouncing the right to hold charges against another.

I would nominate the words that Jesus spoke on the cross as among the most significant words ever spoken: "*Father, forgive them, for they do not know what they are doing*" (Luke 23:24, emphasis mine).

Why would a suffering, dying Jesus say this? After all, no one was asking for His forgiveness, and if any had heard these words, they would have, in their anger at Him, screamed at Him all the louder.

So why did He pray this prayer? With these words, in which He asks God to forgive them, He, in fact, is forgiving them. Why? My opinion? *He did it first for His own sake.*

Perhaps it sounds offensive to say "if I could get into the head of Jesus . . ." but I'll take the risk. If I could get into the head of Jesus, I'll bet I'd find that He was aware that forgiving his enemies was a proactive defense against any temptation to become embittered toward them. If we embrace the truth that Jesus was fully God and fully man and thus capable of facing all temptations (as is said in the book of Hebrews), then I think we're watching a Savior who is protecting Himself against the temptation of hatred and resentment.

Jesus did not wait until angry feelings began to cripple His soul; He chose to proactively forgive (or pray for their forgiveness) so that He could remain the sinless Christ who could die for the sins of the world.

A few years ago I had the privilege of having a personal introduction to Nelson Mandela. It is one of the most memorable moments of my life. Not because I am a hero-worshiper, but because of the experience I had in his presence. When he entered the room and joined one other person and myself, I felt as if I was being enveloped in a cloud of grace. The man simply projected a spiritual force that left me dumbfounded.

Years before meeting Mandela, I had interviewed a man who had been imprisoned with him on Robben Island for five years. "We had rooms [cells] next to each other," he told me.

"What did he teach you?" I asked.

"He taught us to forgive," came the answer. "I was a bitter young man, and Mandela picked it up immediately when we first met. He said to me, 'Son, you are of no use to our movement until you learn to forgive the white man. You can hate his cause, but you cannot hate him.'"

When I was privileged to meet Nelson Mandela, I felt that gracious power that accounted for his splendid resilience. To come from twenty-seven years of imprisonment (the majority of his adulthood) and walk into the light and challenge the South African people—white and black—to forgive was the single most important thing that saved a nation from catastrophic bloodshed.

I return to Claypool's story of two brothers who spent twenty years trapped in resentment. What a loss! And I look at the world in which I live: its lawsuits, its road rage, its vicious mind-killing gossip, its suicide bombers and terrorists, and everything in between. Is it just too simplistic to say forgiveness is a large part of the answer?

No, because granting forgiveness is part of how we repair our pasts, and it's one more of the things that leads to resilience.

SIXTEEN

RESILIENT PEOPLE OVERFLOW WITH GRATITUDE

One night, Gail and I took our grandchildren and their parents to one of those large pizza restaurants where the food is awful but the play area of games and rides is wonderful. Everyone had a great time.

When it came time to leave, one of the grandchildren was strapped into a safety seat in the back of our Outback station wagon. In the process his mother said, "Now, make sure you tell Papa how thankful you are." There was no response.

She said it again. "I want you to tell Papa thank you for the nice evening." Nothing.

She tried a third time. Still nothing.

"It's OK," I said. A frustrated mother sighed, shut the door, and headed for her car.

When we were alone, I decided it was time for a bit of grandfatherly coaching. "You know," I said, "Papa loves to do things for his grandchildren. But it takes the fun out of it if they aren't thankful." I thought this was a reasoned way to address the problem of ingratitude. Logic suggested that there would be an immediate outpouring of thankfulness. But my comments were met with more silence. So it was time for me to get irritated.

My voice raised a decibel or two. "Did you hear what I said?"

"Yep," came the reply.

"You heard me say how important it is to be thankful?"

"Yep."

"Then don't you think it might be a smart idea to say a thank you?" A bit more silence.

Then this: "I am thankful . . . I just don't want to say it."

In the letter to Roman Christians, Paul explained the spiritual condition of societies and cultures where morality and civility break down. Speaking of peoples where there is defiance against God, he wrote, "For although they knew God, they neither glorified him as God nor *gave thanks to him* (Rom. 1:21, emphasis mine).

Two issues mark decadent societies according to Paul: an unwillingness to acknowledge (or honor) the Creator, and a resistance to gratitude. To put this second idea in words our grandson can understand, the human race just doesn't want to say thanks. By nature none of us really wants to.

Yet this is a primary mark of resilient people as they look into their pasts. They seek for things that call for gratitude. They give thanks to people who have made a difference in their lives. Thanks to God for benefits and blessings that they discover are numberless. Thanks in general that one receives the gift of life and thought and beauty and a thousand other things.

The subject of gratitude is such a common one that it is easily passed by as something one might call a no-brainer. Everyone, almost everyone anyway, knows that a few thank-yous here and there work wonders in social relationships.

The clerk in the store hands us our purchases and says, "Thanks;

have a good day." The airline's flight attendant thanks us for flying
with her company. The pastor thanks us for coming to worship. Even
the synthesized voice at the ATM says thank you when we step up for
service. The fact is that we hear the words *thank you* so many times
a day that we often forget about the significance of what is actually
happening.

While the words of gratitude are important—when sincerely
offered—the heart of gratitude is what marks a resilient person. Big
difference!

Ten men with leprosy met Jesus on the road between Galilee and
Samaria. Because custom demanded that they keep their distance,
they could only cry out, "Have pity on us!" Whether they were seeking alms or knew of Jesus' reputation for healing is not known. *Pity*
is their admission that they are desperate for whatever charity
another person might provide.

"Go, show yourselves to the priests" is Jesus' response. Perhaps
more was said than this, but this is all we have of the story. As they
went, Scripture says, "they were cleansed" (Luke 17:14).

> One of them, when he saw he was healed, came back, prais-
> ing God in loud voice. He threw himself at Jesus' feet and
> thanked him—and he was a Samaritan. (vv. 15–16)

"Where are the other nine?" Jesus asked. "Was no one found to
return and give praise to God except this foreigner?" (vv. 17–18).
Jesus is making a point: gratitude is important to Him.

The story is there for one reason: to underscore the importance
of gratitude as the completion of the experience. The other nine—
presumably Jews—should have known better. The only one that
knew enough to be grateful was a Samaritan, and because of the
antipathy between the two cultures, that must have riled any Jews
who stood with Jesus watching all of this.

Two sets of words are underlined in my Bible: "he came back," and "Where are the other nine?" Gratitude is "coming back" to the scene of the event and acknowledging what has happened and who made it happen. It is what the resilient person does as he sweeps his memory for recent and not-so-recent events where there is a need for saying thank you.

We can all remember being taught as children to say thank you. It is one of the first marks of courtesy we hear about. I don't ever remember anyone telling me why it was important say thank you other than the practical reality: *if you're not thankful, people are not likely to continue their generosity toward you.*

The thankful spirit—the intent beneath the words—is the result of continuous discipline, because gratefulness isn't a natural or instinctive thing for most of us. Perhaps the fact that nine of the ten never came back illustrates this. Thankfulness is a learned transaction, and it comes with the realization that I neither deserve nor am entitled to blessings. At best, I am a graced recipient of all I have and am.

Somewhere in his writings, Thomas Kelly said:

We pray for the big things and forget to give thanks for the ordinary, small (and yet really not small) gifts. How can God entrust great things to one who will not thankfully receive from Him the little things?

The old cowboy doffs his hat and says, "Much obliged," as an expression of gratitude. *I'm obligated to you,* he is saying. The words imply humility: that I cannot get along by myself. They imply reliance: that I need the people around me, that I need God. They imply value: that I recognize the cost involved in the giving. And the words imply gladness: that my life has been filled with the joy that comes when human beings connect in gracious ways.

That's why one hears in the vocabulary of resilient people words like *appreciate, grateful, and indebted.* They are used to complete transactions with one another, and, of course, in expressions of worship to God.

On another day, perhaps six months after our evening together at the pizza store, the same grandson was with me again. We had gone to New York City for a day and a night. We'd indulged ourselves in junk food, a visit to the Empire State Building, a ride to the Statue of Liberty, and other exciting things one can do in New York. We were finally on our way home.

He had been still for a while, and I thought he had fallen asleep. But then he spoke.

"Papa?"

"Yeah?"

"Thanks for all the fun we had."

"You're welcome. I enjoyed it too."

"Papa?"

"Yeah?"

"I sure hope you don't die soon, because I want to have a lot more fun like today."

This is all I need to hear. A child has scanned his past—his most recent past—and brought closure to it with gratitude. This time he's said it. And if he will do that sort of thing for the rest of his life, he, too, will be a resilient person.

SEVENTEEN

RESILIENT PEOPLE SQUEEZE THE PAST FOR ALL ITS WISDOM

When I travel someplace to give a talk, I carry as little luggage as possible. That's why I am accustomed to washing shirts, socks, or underwear if I am staying in a hotel somewhere.

Part of this process involves wringing as much water out of wet things as possible so that they will dry quickly. But no matter how hard I try to get rid of every drop of water, it seems as if I can return an hour later and find more to wring out if I try again.

I have this picture in mind as I write about the fourth way resilient people comb the past keeping it all in a state of good repair. For just as I wring out my clothes, so the resilient person wrings out the events in his or her life in order to drain them of all the wisdom they have to offer. In other words, the resilient person is a reflective person. He or she always looks underneath events, seeking their significance.

This is what Mary, the mother of our Lord, did at the time of Jesus' birth. In telling the Christmas story, we love to describe the shepherds who visited the manger scene and then rushed to the streets to "spread the word concerning what had been told them about this child" (Luke 2:17). It sounds exactly like what we've been taught to do: *spread the word*. Mary, however, was quiet.

> But Mary treasured up all these things and pondered them in her heart. (v. 19)

This is the picture of one who takes the time to wring out events and test them for insight and wisdom. Sooner or later, Mary may have something to say, but when she says it, her words will have substance. In days to come, Mary and her small family will face tremendous pressure as Herod's thugs descend upon Bethlehem, seeking her baby's life. She and Joseph will have to flee the country and live as exiles for a while. All of this will demand courage, depth of spirit, and trust in the purposes of God. That's what comes to a person, like Mary, who takes the time to collect wisdom concerning the event.

I find it interesting that we never heard of the shepherds again. Their enthusiasm disappears from the biblical account. But Mary, the reflective one, is always there through the best and worst of moments. And this is typical of wise people. They develop resilience.

Having humiliated myself in the losing of a race I should have won, I hear Coach Goldberg say to me, "I want you to come back on Monday and tell me what you think happened." He is asking me to wring out the event for the lessons it has to offer. If I return to the track on Monday with a clear insight as to where my thinking went wrong, and if I return with an understanding of how I am going to avoid ever doing such a thing again, he will be pleased. I will have acquired a bit of wisdom. Doubtless, he'll make sure that I wrap it in a principle that will stay with me as long as I live.

Which is exactly what happened. I apply the principles of that blown race almost every day of my life. The defeat was not wasted.

Who doesn't equate the ancient King Solomon with the subject of wisdom? His story is a warning to everyone.

When David, Solomon's father, turned the kingdom over to his son, Solomon was smart enough to know that his ability to run the country in the footsteps of his father would require more than charisma or political savvy. Thus his prayer to God:

"I am only a little child and do not know how to carry out my duties. Your servant is here among the people you have chosen, a great people, too numerous to count or number. So give your servant a discerning heart to govern your people and to distinguish between right and wrong. For who is able to govern this great people of yours?" (1 Kings 3:7–9)

Every indication is that God was delighted with Solomon's request. In part, He said:

"I will do what you have asked. I will give you a wise and discerning heart, so that there will never have been anyone like you, nor will there ever be." (v. 12)

Following this promise, the reader gets to see Solomon's wisdom in action. Not only can one read of the building of the fabulous temple, but one is also offered a sample of Solomon's adjudication of a dispute between two prostitutes, each the mother of a son. The two women faced the king with a dilemma. The son of one was dead. Now both claimed the surviving child.

Solomon asked for a sword and commanded that the child be cut in two, a half to be given to each mother. His seemingly calloused ruling elicited two distinct behaviors from the women. From the false mother: a gleam of satisfaction. From the real mother a howl of protest, even a willingness to surrender the child in order that it might live. Solomon, recognizing a mother's instincts, instantly resolved the case.

The episode quickly spread across Israel and became what businesspeople call *a company story,* a tale that typified the ways of a leader.

> When all Israel heard the verdict the king had given, they held the king in awe, because they saw that he had wisdom from God to administer justice. (1 Kings 3:28)

The story of Solomon, however, took a strange turn, for while the man dealt with national affairs with great wisdom, he seemed to conduct his own life in a way that is reminiscent of impulse and compulsion. That this split between wise public conduct and personal stupidity could exist always impresses me.

Centuries before, Moses had warned (see Deuteronomy 17) that a king should never accumulate large amounts of silver and gold, many wives (lest they lead his heart astray), or a huge inventory of horses. This list is reflective of the traditional *money, sex, power* trilogy that undermines strong leaders.

For all of his wisdom in guiding national affairs, Solomon ignored this principle and did just the opposite in his private life. "Solomon was greater in riches and wisdom than all the other kings of the earth" (1 Kings 10:23). In admiration for his wisdom as a national leader, people far and wide deluged Solomon with gifts until his hoarded wealth exceeded the imagination. "Solomon accumulated chariots and horses" (v. 26). And then, finally, Solomon "loved many foreign women" (11:1).

Everything that Moses had once warned about materialized in the king's life, and "the LORD became angry with Solomon because his heart had turned away from the LORD, the God of Israel, who had appeared to him twice" (11:9).

Somewhere along the line, Solomon stopped wringing the past

for its insights. The *present* in life became all-important, and he became dominated by his instincts. The man stopped listening, stopped asking for right things, stopped seeing his position as a stewardship.

To wring things out . . . to squeeze events for meaning . . . to acquire insight and wisdom: How is this done?

While I offer the disclaimer that I do not perceive myself as an eminently wise man, I can describe my own personal pursuit of wisdom.

Number one, I've learned to ask questions. First of myself and then of others. Years ago I heard Peter Drucker say to a group of young leaders, "Always ask about the things you are seeing, '*What does this mean?*'" It was a simple but profound instruction. Never go beyond something of note without asking, *what is to be learned here? Why was there success or failure? How could this have been done in a better way? What did this cost, and will the benefits justify the expense?*

Second, I've been impressed with a principle that separates mediocre chess players from the great ones: always be looking four, maybe five, moves ahead of the present one. *Where does this lead? What are the possible unintended consequences? Where in my past (or anyone's past that I know about) is there precedent for what has happened? What decisions or choices lie ahead as a result of what has happened?*

Wise people look at yesterday and ask how it will affect tomorrow. They are aware that most things are interconnected, that things lead to other things. Wisdom comes in figuring out where things are going.

Time and again I find myself talking to people whose lives appear to be lived purely on the surface. "Have you thought about . . . ?" No, they haven't. "Well, what do you think this will do to . . . ?" They have no idea. "Does it ever occur to you that . . . ?" No, not really. "Have you ever asked yourself what God . . . ?" Never thought of that.

Jesus went out as usual to the Mount of Olives, and his disciples followed him. On reaching the place, he said to them,
"Pray that you will not fall into temptation." He withdrew
about a stone's throw beyond them, knelt down and prayed.
(Luke 22:39–41)

Believers know the full story. Jesus prayed; the disciples slept.
Result: when their enemies came, Jesus acted with full dignity; the
disciples panicked and ran. He acted out of wisdom; they, out of
instinct.

It is Exhibit A of the difference between one who knows how to
wring from his past all the insight and power needed for the moment
and the others who have no idea about what is happening at all.
Resilient people know that difference.

⸿ IV. ⸞

RESILIENT PEOPLE TRAIN TO GO THE DISTANCE

They prepare themselves for the "emergencies" of life.

They know exactly what has to be accomplished.

They keep themselves physically fit.

They grow their minds.

They harness their emotions.

They trim their egos.

They open their hearts to the presence of God.

SPRINT OR GO THE DISTANCE

The Penn Relays (first held in 1895) rank as one of the greatest annual track meets in the world. Each April, thousands of runners descend on Franklin Field in Philadelphia to compete for ribbons, medals, and trophies. I ran for Stony Brook in the Penn Relays for three consecutive years.

The grandstands were full on one of those race days when I walked to the starting line with my starting blocks. I had been selected to be the leadoff runner for the Stony Brook team in a prep-school mile relay race. Our team (four runners each running a lap) had drawn the number-two lane, and the team from Poly Prep in Brooklyn (one of our perennial rivals) had drawn number one.

When the leadoff runner from Poly Prep appeared, I recognized him. He had recently set a 100-meter dash record for prep-school runners. We nodded to each other, each, perhaps, sensing that the interior race was between us and would not necessarily include the other six runners from other schools.

The team managers provided both of us with wooden mallets to pound the front and rear spikes of the starting blocks into the ground. Finished, we straightened up and removed our sweat togs. When our eyes met again, the runner from Poly Prep said, "May the best man win. I'll be waiting for you at the finish line." Today we would refer to this as trash talk.

A race official gave each of the eight starters a baton. Then we heard the familiar words of the starter: "Runners, take your marks!" Each of us made one more attempt to loosen up and control the surge of adrenaline now surging through our bodies. Then we carefully, deliberately, stepped over the starting blocks and began to assume the runners' starting position. Everything had to be perfect: spikes pressed against the blocks, fingers spread and planted on the track, the rest of the body coiled, ready to spring.

"Set," the starting judge called out. Eight rear ends raised upward; eight pairs of eyes stared straight down the running lanes toward the first turn.

Crack! It was the sharp report of the starter's pistol. All eight of us burst into action and began that smooth 30-meter rise from the starting crouch to the streamlined position of the runner in full stride. Instantly the crowd came to life.

I remember thinking how quickly the man from Poly Prep disappeared. He was gone! And I recall feeling the sensation of cinders kicked up by his spikes hitting my shins. We had not even reached the first turn, and I was already thinking of a second-place position in the handoff box when I would hand off the baton to Stony Brook's second man.

We charged around the first turn and into the straightaway. Ahead was the man from Poly Prep, way ahead. I was in second place, a meter or two ahead of the others. Now we were halfway down the straightaway. And then, suddenly, I realized that the man from Poly Prep was slowing down. Quickly I caught him and flew past.

Now I was entering the back turn, my arms thrashing, knees high. Coming off the turn, I went into the kick, that final burst that came from months of speed and endurance training. I could see Stony Brook's number-two man in the handoff box just ahead, and he was beginning to run, looking over his right shoulder so that he could gauge my speed. Then when I was two meters behind him, he turned to look straight ahead, his right hand extended behind him, his thumb and forefinger forming a large V. Now it was my responsibility to catch him and set the baton squarely into his V-shaped hand. When I did, I could feel him close his grip on the baton. I released it, and he was gone. Curving off onto the infield, I ran to the other side of the track where I could cheer him on when he came around the first turn.

I forgot to see what happened to the man from Poly Prep.

"Gordie, come here, please." It was the tenor voice of Marvin Goldberg, somehow easily heard above the crowd's noise. We stood together and watched the race continue until all four runners from each team had completed their legs of the relay race and it was over.

Goldberg seemed unconcerned about whether Stony Brook had won the race or not. He preferred to talk. "I heard what he said to you, and I want you to remember that moment for the rest of your life. I want you to bear in mind that it makes little difference how fast you run a 100-meter event if the race is 400 meters long. Today you ran the total distance; he ran only a sprint."

The coach had taught me something important about resilience. Too many people see life as a sprint—something fast, furious, quickly finished, bereft of any deep breathing. But life is more than a burst of speed. It is a distance run, and it demands endurance, determination, and a kick at the finish.

That all comes from one source: *the pursuit of self-mastery . . . discipline.*

EIGHTEEN

RESILIENT PEOPLE PREPARE THEMSELVES FOR THE "EMERGENCIES" OF LIFE

Everyone who competes in the games goes into strict training.
—PAUL THE APOSTLE (1 COR. 9:25)

Neil Bascomb has written a wonderful book called *The Perfect Mile.* In it he tells the story of Roger Bannister, John Landy, and Wes Santee, three athletes who committed themselves to breaking the four-minute mile. Bascomb writes:

> All three runners endured thousands of hours of training to shape their bodies and minds. They ran more miles in a year than many of us walk in a lifetime. They spent a large part of their youth struggling for breath. They trained week after week to the point of collapse, all to shave off a second, maybe two, during a mile race—the time it takes to snap one's fingers and register the sound. There were sleepless nights and training sessions in rain, sleet, snow, and scorching heat.

There were times when they wanted to go out for a beer or a date yet knew they couldn't. They understood that life was somehow different for them, that idle happiness eluded them. If they weren't training or racing or gathering the will required for these efforts, they were trying not to think about training or racing at all.[1]

The term some have used to describe what these men were doing is *self-mastery*. Others prefer the word *discipline*. Some athletes would be happy with *conditioning*. Each of them describes the attempt to push oneself beyond the ordinary and achieve something unique and extraordinarily satisfying.

When we speak of disciplining a child, we mean the process of bringing a young human being into alignment with standards of conviction and behavior that are not necessarily natural to human nature. The disciplinary process includes teaching, modeling, and correction all within a caring and loving *but firm* context. The end result we seek is referred to as *maturity*.

And coaches do much the same thing as a parent does to a child and a landscaper to a sapling. The Old Testament reflects on the process with the words "Train [or "discipline"] a child in the way he should go, and when he is old he will not turn from it" (Prov. 22:6).

At the beginning of this book I related Marvin Goldberg's words to me as an aspiring runner: "I think you have the potential to be an excellent runner . . . but you have much to learn. If you are to compete for Stony Brook, you're going to have to work hard, discipline yourself. You will have to trust me and follow my instructions. Every day you will have to come to this track and complete the workouts that will be assigned to you. Don't commit to this if you are not willing to give it everything you have."

Goldberg was introducing me to discipline, a concept I had never before fully appreciated. His opening message: that the rewards we seek in life begin with submission to discipline and training.

Looking back, I realize that all the way through my childhood there were others that were teaching me the ways of discipline. I just never understood it until Marvin Goldberg spelled it out for me.

My parents had tried, insisting, for example, that I do certain chores around our home. And not just *do* them, but do them with excellence. One day after I had supposedly dusted the furniture in our home, my father called me over to the small grand piano in our living room. The late afternoon sun was shining through the window, and its rays exposed the fact that I had given the piano's top little more than a cursory swipe or two with the rag. The undusted surface was like a revealed fingerprint. And the evidence there was indisputable: I hadn't done the job.

My father pointed to the dust and said, "Do you want people to come into our home, look at this, and assume that this is the way your family does its work? The quality of *your* work reflects on all of us." Why this moment remains with me more than fifty years later is something I find difficult to understand. But I recall it often when I'm tempted to leave something unfinished or poorly done. *The quality of your work reflects on all of us.*

To set goals and make things happen do not come easily or automatically, but only to the person who pushes him- or herself to higher standards and greater achievements. And this began to make sense under the coaching of Marvin Goldberg. I began to see that each day we make a stream of choices, saying no to certain things and yes to others. And our willingness to do this creates a growing stamina that makes it possible to do more, know more, serve more a day later.

Remember Daniel? Early in life I absorbed the story of him and his three friends, who spent most of their youth in the training academies of a Babylonian emperor. They were young men, the storyteller says, "without any physical defect, handsome, showing aptitude for every kind of learning, well informed, quick to understand, and qualified to serve in the king's palace" (Dan. 1:4).

They were there to learn the "language and literature of the Babylonians." And the Scripture adds, "The king assigned them a daily amount of food and wine" (v. 5).

> But Daniel resolved not to defile himself with the royal food and wine. (v. 8)

There was consternation on the part of those responsible for the development of these men. They weren't about to let any of their protégés become unhealthy or unattractive.

"Please test [*discipline* could fit here] your servants," Daniel said, "for ten days: Give us nothing but vegetables to eat and water to drink. Then compare our appearance with that of the young men who eat the royal food, and treat your servants in accordance with what you see" (vv. 12–13).

At the end of the testing period, it was clear that "they looked healthier and better nourished than any of the young men who ate the royal food" (v. 15).

The lesson of the story? Here were young men who were learning not to indulge themselves but rather to make austere, will-enforcing choices that would build the stamina of their interior lives. And it paid off.

Thomas Merton wrote:

> No one who simply eats or drinks when he feels like eating or drinking or smokes whenever he feels the urge to light a cigarette, or gratifies his curiosity and sensuality whenever they are stimulated, can consider himself a free person. He has renounced his spiritual freedom and become the ser-

vant of bodily impulse. Therefore his mind and his will are not fully his own. They are under the power of his appetites, and through the medium of his appetites they are under the control of those who gratify his appetites.[2]

Merton offers an idea that seems paradoxical: *We are most free when we are under discipline.* This is something that more than a few moderns do not understand. They exalt freedom as the notion that one can do anything he or she wants at any time. And yet no one is freer than the person whose mind, body, and soul are conditioned to grow and flourish.

Elton Trueblood wrote:

Acceptance of discipline is the price of freedom. The pole vaulter is not free to go over the high bar except as he disciplines himself rigorously day after day. The freedom of the surgeon to use his drill to cut away the bony structure, close to a tiny nerve without severing it, arises from a similar discipline.

It is doubtful if excellence in any field comes in any other way. John Milton was revealing something of his own creative power when he wrote, "There is nothing in the world of more grave and urgent importance throughout the whole life of man than is discipline.[3]

Many people would love to have their names on the cover of a book. Admittedly, it is a marvelous feeling of accomplishment. But no one except the writer knows of the lonely hours spent before a keyboard testing thoughts and concepts through words on a page. The joy, the freedom that comes with the finished product is exhilarating. But the road of disciplinary activity that led to the finished product is fraught with struggle.

As I moved into my university years, I began to meet people who took self-mastery very seriously. When I joined the University of Colorado track team, I met Bill Toomey, who, a few years later, would become the Decathlon gold medal winner for the United States in Mexico City. We often walked to the track together and began the workouts that Coach Frank Potts had designed for us. When a workout was over, I would slink back to the locker room, exhausted, anxious to get showered, dressed, and on my way home.

But Toomey would remain at the track, rest a short while, and repeat the workout a second time. Before long there was a significant gap between his performances on the track and mine. And when I tell this story (which I often have), I say, "Now you understand why everyone in the world of amateur athletics has heard the name of Bill Toomey, but no one—no one!—has ever heard the name of Gordon MacDonald."

The difference began in the area of discipline. Looking back on his greatest athletic years, Toomey said:

> Whatever pursuit you undertake, the requirements should start with a love of what it is that you are pursuing. Once you have selected a sport or a creative activity, the rules are pretty much the same. One of the key elements is the ability to be honest with yourself. Too many athletes do not admit their weaknesses. In order to continue achieving, one must have discipline and adhere to a program. Many athletes do not have a well thought out map on where they are going and how they will ultimately get there.[4]

During my university days I began to meet scholars, artists, and researchers who would have thoroughly agreed with Toomey. They were men and women who were prepared to work or study long into the night, submit themselves to harsh critique, and experiment a hundred times (and often fail) in order to achieve the breakthrough on the 101st time. I was awed by their tenacity, their concentration, their determination to wave off all superfluous distractions. I'd never seen intensity like that.

And then, when I could appreciate them, I began to meet saints. People of faith—usually much older—who deserved the phrase used in the Bible about such people, "the world was not worthy of them."

In terms of discipline, their conditioning was the spiritual kind: extended times of prayer, reflection, Scripture study, sacrificial service, and even suffering that was absent of complaining. I met people who gladly accepted the discipline of poverty, severe living conditions, submission to systems (and people) that were unjust and oppressive. But in spite of it all, their souls seemed to shine, and every word they spoke, every action they took, seemed to make a difference. In their presence I felt lifted toward God, and I felt a gentle persuasion to climb higher myself.

And I said of the athletes, the scholars, the saints, *"I want to be like them."*

Now I know that the doorway to resilience is marked with discipline or self-mastery. I am at that moment in life when the temptations increase to slough off responsibility, to freeze-frame old ideas, to resist change, to let someone else do the heavy lifting. But I will not do that, because the disciplines I've learned over the years will not let me. And I like it that way.

During the days of graduate school when I studied theology, I came under the influence of an ex-missionary whose name was Raymond Buker. He and his wife had given the large part of their lives to work in Burma. During much of their lives they had suffered intensely as they obeyed what they believed to be the call of God to the indigenous people of that part of the world. Perhaps one of the reasons I was drawn to Raymond Buker was that he had represented the United States in the 1924 Olympic Games in Paris, the games made famous by the running of Eric Liddle of *Chariots of Fire.*

Dr. Buker was a man of deep character, a godly man, but not so serious that he couldn't laugh with the heartiest of us. He was also the epitome of self-mastery. I offered to buy him a cup of coffee one day. He told me he would enjoy joining me for conversation, but the coffee would be unnecessary.

"No coffee?" I said. "You've got to have your morning coffee."

"No thanks. I just appreciate the conversation."

After several exchanges of this type over the next weeks when I would offer Buker coffee and he would graciously refuse, I said, "You must really dislike coffee."

"No, as a matter of fact, I like coffee very much."

"Then . . ."

"A long time ago I learned the importance of regularly practicing saying no to myself. And sometimes that means saying no to things that I like. Coffee is one of them. And each time I say no to coffee, I remind myself that there may come a day when I have to say a very serious 'no' to other things of much greater importance. And I'll have practiced on simpler things . . . like your cup of coffee."

Spoken like a resilient person.

NINETEEN

RESILIENT PEOPLE KNOW EXACTLY WHAT HAS TO BE ACCOMPLISHED

One hundred years ago, self-mastery was a popular subject. People thrilled to the stories of nineteenth- and early-twentieth-century explorers—Perry, Byrd, Shackleton, and Scott come to mind—and their willingness to push themselves to the limits of human endurance. Today there seems to be a far greater emphasis on the glamour of achievement rather than the grittiness of it.

Still, there are those who tell the story of self-discipline and what it takes to go beyond the boundary of the normal. Jamie Clark writes of preparing to climb Mt. Everest:

> When you get yourself in shape for a climb, you spend several hours a day working on an inclined treadmill with a heavy pack on your back. You look goofy. You smell. It's an ugly scene. That's always true. The road to success is not pretty.

Resilient people know this, and it does not alarm them. They seek the satisfaction of knowing that every part of their lives is under personal control, and they understand that there is a price to be paid for this.

They understand the words of Peter, who wrote:

Prepare your minds for action; be self-controlled; set your hope fully on the grace to be given you when Jesus Christ is revealed. As obedient children, do not conform to the evil desires you had when you lived in ignorance. But just as he who called you is holy, so be holy in all you do. (1 Pet. 1:13–15)

Early Christians learned that crisis might be around any corner, that they might be called upon to answer for their convictions even to the point of imprisonment and martyrdom. In the account of his sufferings, Paul speaks of being beaten five times in the so-called heresy trial where the guilty party was stripped to the waist, stretched over a rack, and mercilessly strapped thirty-nine times. It is recorded that more than a few people died under such duress; others in their humiliation ended their own lives. Paul faced this kind of ordeal five times.

Only disciplined people could withstand such suffering. And that meant that they conditioned themselves day by day so that they were tough enough if and when the critical moment came.

"Everyone who competes in the games goes into strict training," Paul wrote. "They do it to get a crown that will not last; but we do it to get a crown that will last forever. Therefore I do not run like a man running aimlessly; I do not fight like a man beating the air. No, I beat my body and make it my slave so that after I have preached to others, I myself will not be disqualified for the prize" (1 Cor. 9:25–27).

My simplest explanation of discipline is to refer to it as *intentional suffering.* It is the act of insisting that the body, the mind, and the spirit engage in challenges that build up capacity and stamina.

This intentional suffering is rarely considered fun. It is not associated with leisure. In the process of disciplining oneself, there is often humiliation and defeat. Gratification and achievement are often postponed for a long time. And the disciplined person does not pursue ways that are likely to make him or her popular. It is only after the season of discipline is over and the payoff comes that the world, standing amazed, offers applause and admiration.

The runner, the wrestler, the swimmer all push their bodies to heightened levels of performance by demanding of themselves longer, faster, and stronger episodes of physical output. They do not stop simply because there is the feeling of fatigue or even pain. They understand that these are mental barriers that have to be overcome. They insist that their bodies behave in accordance with willpower and not simple convenience.

The same, of course, can be said for the follower of Christ who responds to a call from heaven to face a herculean task.

A friend of mine, Retired Admiral Tim Ziemer, relates the story of his mother and father, who were missionaries in Vietnam during the Vietnamese war. One day while under attack by Vietcong, they, along with a number of wounded Vietnamese, hid in a bunker. When the attack became intolerable, my friend's father dared to leave the bunker and approach the enemy to ask for a truce so that the wounded and dying could be evacuated. But the minute he was seen, the Vietcong shot him dead. His wife, my friend's mother, watched this happen.

> While my father was negotiating for permission to take the injured to a local provincial hosptital, he was shot. My mother was hiding in the bunker and didn't actually see him shot. After she was ordered out of the bunker at gunpoint,

she saw my father lying in the dust of the mission com-
pound. She was forced to walk past his body without being
able to go to him to render assistance, check on his conditio
or touch him in a gesture of farewell.

Later, when the Vietcong released Mrs. Ziemer to a Vietnamese
hospital, a nurse said to her, "You must hate our nation and our
people." Her response to the nurse was, "No, I don't hate your country, nor do I hate your people. I love your country and your people,
and I came to your country to tell you about a God who gives me
that love through a man named Jesus."

A reply of this sort is not manufactured in the moment. It comes
as the result of inner spiritual discipline year after year, day after day.
Her resilience continues.

The other day Admiral Ziemer's mother—now a very aged
woman—wrote to him and said, "Son, consider yourself the least,
consider yourself the littlest and put yourself last . . . others always
first." Reflecting on her words, Tim said, "I learned a long time ago
to listen to my mom! I've been privileged to sit under some profound preaching and teaching; my library is full of books on how to
live out my Christian life, but as I look back, it's been the living of the
word through my mother's life that has done as much as anyone to
show me what knowing the Savior as her own is all about . . . to be
whole and complete in Him . . . to lean on Him . . . to trust Him for
all her needs."

"We live our lives under the discipline of uncertainty," an
English Christian leader, Fred Mitchell, said:

We never know what emergencies may be approaching,
what (opportunities) may be ripening, what chances may be
on the way, what temptations (may be lying in) ambush
ready to spring unawares.

When a person seeks the unique resilience of a Christian view of life, he or she she does it with some of the following things in mind.

Discipline strengthens the will. It enlarges the capacity of a person to summon courage when life gets tough. This is what one sees when Daniel's three friends—Shadrach, Meshach, and Abednego—refused to bow down before a pagan idol and were threatened with immolation in the so-called fiery furnace. Their response in the face of certain death:

> "We do not need to defend ourselves before you in this matter. If we are thrown into the blazing furnace, the God we serve is able to save us from it, and he will rescue us from your hand, O king. But even if he does not, we want you to know, O king, that we will not serve your gods or worship the image of gold you have set up." (Dan. 3:16–18)

These ancient stories are the bedrock of biblical faith. They speak of brave men and women who took their God so seriously that they were not intimidated by such pressure. All of their lives they toughened themselves through discipline in order to face such a supreme moment of test. Their willpower was up to the occasion because they'd disciplined themselves.

But where did the willpower of Daniel's friends come from? I suspect we saw it first in the story of their refusal to eat and drink excessively in their years at the training academy. This was merely the extension of lives earlier disciplined to say yesses and noes at the right moments.

Discipline brings the spiritual gifts and skills of a person to the highest possible level of effectiveness. "How do you get to Carnegie Hall?" asks the tourist of a New Yorker. Answer: "You practice, man; you practice."

Discipline develops stamina. Is there a story in the Bible better known than the one about David and Goliath? The young boy, David, volunteered to go out onto the field of battle and face the Philistine giant. Saul seemed to be happy to let the kid do his best, but he had grave doubts about the possibility of success. "You are not able to go out against this Philistine and fight him," he said. "You are only a boy, and he has been a fighting man from his youth" (1 Sam. 17:33).

But David expresses a confidence based upon the disciplines of his life.

> "Your servant has been keeping his father's sheep. When a lion or a bear came and carried off a sheep from the flock, I went after it, struck it and rescued the sheep from its mouth. When it turned on me, I seized it by its hair, struck it and killed it. Your servant has killed both the lion and the bear; this uncircumcised Philistine will be like one of them . . . The LORD who delivered me from the paw of the lion and the paw of the bear will deliver me from the hand of this Philistine." (vv. 34–37)

Self-mastery breeds confidence of spirit and strength in skill. Each effort builds toward the next. Having used this selection to illustrate my point, I would be remiss, however, if I ignored David's own awareness that behind his development and physical ability was the delivering strength of God, who graciously undergirded his efforts.

Finally, discipline produces excellence in life and work. By doing things regularly and repetitively, one acquires the ability to do something far more effectively and in a way that inspires others.

I see Paul living this way with respect to the development of the men around him. And because he disciplined himself to an excellent way of life, he could confidently say to Timothy, "You . . . know all about my teaching, my way of life, my purpose, faith, patience, love, endurance, persecutions, sufferings . . ." (2 Tim. 3:10). And he could say this with such confidence because he knew he had disciplined himself to give his best in all of those sectors of life. Now the modeling of that life was Timothy's to have as a gift in the building of his own faith and character. All of his life, Timothy would have something to copy—a straight-edge of excellent living. No better gift.

When Charles Eliot was president of Harvard University, he was asked to name the most important quality a leader of a university needed. His answer: "the capacity to inflict pain." Eliot understood that if an institution was to grow and to achieve its mission with excellence, there had to be times of pain—the discipline that comes with calling people to reach their potential and, perhaps, even go beyond.

When I read Eliot's words, I thought of Coach Goldberg. He was willing to inflict a kind of pain (or so his runners perceived it). He pushed us beyond levels of fatigue and exhaustion, and we thought him a cruel taskmaster. There were more than a few times, I must confess, when we muttered hateful things behind his back. But those times were during the practices. On the days of track and cross-country competition, it was another story. When our teams piled up one victory after another and collected our medals and trophies, we forgot our occasional hostilities and loved him for pushing us to do out best. Had he permitted, we would have carried him to the team bus on our shoulders. He had made us learn to labor and reap the fruit of self-mastery.

It seems to me that resilient people understand in a strange way that it is important to inflict pain upon themselves. To demand that extra something from the body, the mind, the soul, that most people do not naturally want to give. And that makes all the difference.

TWENTY

RESILIENT PEOPLE KEEP THEMSELVES PHYSICALLY FIT

Tradition says that Saint Paul was neither a large nor a particularly healthy man. I imagine him as an envious spectator at the games, wishing he could compete. I see him watching the victors as they approached the judges' stand to receive the wreaths of victory. Perhaps he dreamed of what it would have been like to be the man of the hour.

> There is no greater glory for a living man
> Than all that he can win by his own feet and hands.
> So come, compete, and from your heart cast care away!

So said the Phaeacian prince, Laodamas, in the *Odyssey*, when he invited Odysseus to come to the Phaeacian games.

"Physical training is of some value," Paul wrote to Timothy (1 Tim. 4:8). Of course, his larger point was that training in the realm of the spiritual was the superior endeavor. But still he recognized that the workouts of an athlete had merit.

When I think of the various disciplines in my own life, I have to start with the physical—the care and development of this "tent" as Paul put it (2 Cor. 5:1). The body is a wondrous physical mechanism formed by God. Cared for properly, it is capable of sustaining life for nine, if not ten, decades. Bodies deserve better than a lot of us are giving them these days.

The Christian movement in which I grew up had little to say about this body of mine. It was a movement so bent on converting the world that it gave scant attention to physical issues and disciplines. "The body is the temple of the Holy Spirit," we often heard when it came time to preach against the use of tobacco and alcohol or against displaying it in a sensual fashion (from 1 Cor. 6:19). But the verse was rarely interpreted to mean anything else.

But that was yesterday; today things have changed, and many of us have come to delight in the mysteries of our physical selves. We focus on the amazing handiwork of God in the complexities of each of the bodily systems. We are awed by the fact that the whole thing works as well as it does and that life is sustained year after year.

Just days ago I watched a very heavy man in his midfifties fall hard to the floor because his heart stopped. Three women—one a nurse, the other two with CPR training—formed a team within seconds and went into action. One began heart compressions, a second started mouth to mouth resuscitation, and a third hooked up a portable defibrillator. The man had stopped breathing, and his pulse was gone. For two or three minutes, he was dead. And then their efforts brought him back to consciousness.

A dozen other men—mostly midlifers—stood in a circle around this unfolding drama, their faces ashen. Many of them were seriously overweight, underexercised men, and you could sense that their feelings were divided between concern for the man on the floor and an awareness that this could happen to them.

I have no doubt that more than a few of them went away from this moment making vows to do something about their own physical conditions.

Some time ago I decided that the care of my body is in fact a high priority and, after a twenty-five year layoff from competitive running, I began to run again. Not competitively, of course, but for my own enjoyment. My physician helped convince me that I was reaching a point in my life at which it was either the discipline of exercise and nutrition or a migration toward medications that were both expensive and fraught with unwanted side effects. Add to that the persuasions of a wife who loves a flat stomach and the idea of a husband who might stay around for a while.

Today, with Gail's encouragement, I am careful (not obsessive) about what I eat and the maintenance of a proper weight level. Each day I budget thirty minutes for running three miles either on the country roads around our home, the treadmill in our basement, or in the fitness center of a hotel, if I am traveling. I try to maintain a schedule of reasonable rest, including midday naps.

People who aspire to resilience take these things seriously. They understand that if they care for their bodies, they have taken a positive step toward a longer and healthier life. It is good common sense, and it fulfills the law of stewardship: what God gives we take care of.

But the discipline of the body is more than a health-giving measure. It is an introit to other disciplines. I have learned that when I push my body for an extended time—as in a three-to-six-mile run—the other pieces of who I am seem to awaken to the fact that I, Gordon, really am the boss and that my entire being is expected to submit to the convictions and intentions I have set in place for myself.

Thomas Kelly once referred to each of us as a "committee of selves," each part of us a bit defiant, each wanting to be chairman of the board (with or without "Gordon"). When I have completed my physical disciplines, I have this sense that the rest of my committee of selves mutter to one another, "Well, he's insisted that the body do what he wants; we may as well accept the fact that he's the chairman and he's going to make us do what he wants too."

Thus, having completed my physical discipline, I am in a much better frame of mind to turn myself toward my spiritual disciplines, toward the day's mind-taxing work activities: writing, preparing talks, solving the problems of organizational leadership. I am better prepared to answer phone calls I'd prefer avoiding and tackling problems that would be easy to put off.

The New Testament is blunt on subjects like self-control and self-discipline. When Paul writes of societies that are unraveling due to moral collapse, one of the issues he raises is that of people without self-control (see 2 Tim. 3:3). When he speaks of a person who is filled with God's Spirit, he notes the evidences of "power, of love, and of self-discipline" (1:7).

This third word in Paul's trilogy of virtues—*self-discipline*—is variously translated from the ancient Greek language as "prudence," or "soundness of mind." It reflects a deep value found in Greek culture where prudence (a moderate mind) was seen as a mark of great maturity and citizenship.

The self-discipline of the body is not a popular subject today. And the Christian community, which should be leading the way in the care and discipline of the body, leaves much to be desired. We are a people who want to be taken seriously in terms of our opinions regarding the sanctity of life, but we are, I'm afraid, rather choosy about what we think that means.

Much too often in such situations I find myself talking with people who are seriously overweight, who admit to sloppy eating habits and to rest patterns that make no sense whatsoever. Imagine a conversation like this:

"Do you respect yourself?"

"Respect myself? . . . I'm not sure. Why do you ask?"

"Are you sure you want to talk about this?"

"Yeah, I'm sure."

"Well, I'm noting the way you appear to take care of your body. It tells me that you enjoy eating more than you enjoy taking good care of yourself. My impression is that a part of you that wants to eat is speaking louder than a part of you that desires to be healthy and vital. Why do you think that is?"

"I'm not sure I know the answer."

"What do you do each day to keep yourself in shape?"

"Well, I've been thinking that I've got to get into an exercise program."

"When do you think that might start?"

"When I'm not so busy."

"My bet is that you probably are struggling with your spiritual disciplines, aren't you?"

"Umm . . . yeah."

"You got room for a couple more cheap shots? How are you doing in the disciplines of spending money? Any struggles with sexual temptation?"

Usually, not always, there are connections, and the other person in this conversation finally acknowledges that large parts of his or her life are out of control.

A reader will be excused if he or she thinks that this is a long series of assumptions built merely on the basis of poor eating habits. But the fact is that there are usually connections all across the board. One breakdown in self-mastery leads to others.

Result? A diminution of resilience.

This is why I have become convinced that the road to self-mastery begins with what I do with my body.

One of the first four-minute milers, Australian John Landy,

recently looked back forty years to the time when he was at his peak. Of his running experiences he said:

> Running gave me discipline and self-expression . . . It has all the disappointments, frustrations, lack of success and unexpected success, which all reproduce themselves in the bigger play of life. It teaches you the ability to present under pressure. It teaches you the importance of being enthusiastic, dedicated, focused. All of these are trite statements, but if you actually have to through these things as a young man, it's very, very important.[1]

As much as I have referred to the life and challenges of the runner, this is not a book about running. Neither is it the theme of this chapter except as it can be seen as an effort to keep our rebellious and defiant bodies under control. And when God's Spirit is in us, one of the evidences is *self-control* seen in our resilient and disciplined bodies.

TWENTY-ONE

RESILIENT PEOPLE GROW THEIR MINDS

———

More than once I have heard the story of President Franklin Roosevelt's 1933 visit to the home of Oliver Wendell Holmes Jr. When the president arrived, the ninety-two-year-old Holmes was sitting in his library reading Plato.

After the two men had settled comfortably, Roosevelt ventured a question: "May I ask you why you're reading Plato, Mr. Justice?"

"Certainly, Mr. President. To improve my mind."

Resilient people believe in a continuously improving mind. Even in their nineties.

The mind is like a muscle. Ignore it, and it becomes flabby. Push it, exercise it, make great demands on it, and it will grow strong and immensely usable.

Stephen, the first Christian martyr, had a remarkable mind. When opponents of the Christian way disputed with him, it is said, "they could not stand up against his wisdom or the Spirit by whom he spoke" (Acts 6:10).

It is quite probable that among those who "disputed" with

Stephen was Saul of Tarsus, a young Pharisee with remarkable intellectual vigor. Even he could not back Stephen down when it came to intellectual confrontation. When the frustration of Saul and others reached a boiling point, they arranged for a set of trumped-up heresy charges that cost Stephen his life.

I was in my early thirties before the issue of a strong mind became a passion for me. It was only then that I began to become aware of intellectual discipline, and I set out to learn how to think. Just as a weight lifter disciplines him- or herself to lift heavier and heavier weights, I had to learn to "lift" heavier ideas.

In Victor Hugo's *Les Miserables*, there is a line regarding the priest, Myriel, who, Hugo says, "was fated to undergo the lot of every newcomer to a little town where there are many mouths that speak, and *but few heads that think*" (emphasis mine).

I came to love watching a thinker in action. And I longed that I might have the ability to join the company of the thinkers. To this day I have this internal image of myself as several cuts below the greater minds that I often mix with on a daily basis. And I have regrets that I did not discipline my mind at an earlier age. But that does not mean that I haven't worked hard to catch up. If I live to be 200, perhaps . . .

The undisciplined mind becomes a lazy mind and easily succumbs to the dominance of another mind. I confess my growing uneasiness at this American Christian world of ours which—thanks to Christian media—is drowning in books, TV programs, and radio where preachers offer systems of thought that are absorbed by the vulnerable listener without the slightest hint of dialogue. Little of value and depth is ever learned through the one-way monologue, be it a sermon or a lecture. And yet there are many eloquent speakers who are relentless in offering their opinions and judgments on just about every issue and who weave a spell of thought that relieves the individual of exploring things for themselves.

The undisciplined mind too easily accepts a blanket ideology that offers a "correct" response for everything. One walks through the Christian community knowing full well that an inappropriate response to a political comment, a doctrinal issue, or a matter of social policy can lose friends, a reputation, even a job. The disciplined, trained mind, however, resists the cookie-cutter approach to thought. It weighs every question and asks if Scripture speaks directly or indirectly to the matter. It weighs it in the light of history: How has the Christian community faced this question before? It measures the matter in terms of its ability to reflect the redeeming love of God. And it asks, will this bring credibility or shame to the Christian movement?

———

It came to me one day that the discipline of the mind was not unlike the conditioning process that Coach Goldberg had put me through month after month as he tried to turn me into a runner. I would have to ensure that, on a regular basis, my mind was being stretched so that it could manage the ever-enlarging ideas that were coming my way as I grew older.

Reading was one form of intellectual discipline. Thankfully, I discovered books in my earliest years, and—introvert that I am—I loved nothing better than to retreat to my bedroom and read.

Today reading is an indispensable part of my life, and I try to keep a balance of old and new books before me. Biographies are at the top of the list. Books that analyze both past and contemporary history are important. Great spiritual classics that open the soul to the presence of God are a significant part of the reading diet.

The mind is disciplined when I deliberately expose myself to people who are better and smarter than me. Why this is difficult for some people and easier for others is a mystery to me. It may be that because I began life with the assumption that everyone was smarter than me, I'm not troubled by the fact that an enormous number of people I meet *are* smarter than me.

In the presence of such people it is wise to become silent and listen.

I love the words of G. K. Chesterton, who said of Abraham Lincoln:

> This great man had one secret vice far more unpopular among his followers than the habit of drinking. He had the habit of thinking. We might almost call it the habit of secret thinking, a dark consolation like that of secret drinking.[1]

You want to cultivate the company of these kinds of people.

The disciplined mind is a master of the questions. Does anyone remember the old *Colombo* TV dramas? Colombo was the magnificent asker of questions. He would cock his head, feigning an expression of confusion, which always disarmed the suspect. His questions seemed to come from everywhere, and, at first, seemed to make no sense.

Colombo might say good-bye and start for the door, which tempted a person to let down his or her guard.

But suddenly, Colombo would turn around and apologize. "Oh . . . [and he might run his fingers through his hair, as if really confused] forgive me . . . must have forgotten something. Did you . . . ?" And the trap would be sprung.

There is an art to asking questions, and relatively few people ever master it. But asking good questions is indeed like being a detective. The questions explore a person's life and thought. They shed light on new ideas. They open up information that can feed the mind and heart.

The disciplined mind follows the arts. What are the writers, the poets, and the artists saying? Where do they see history going?

I make sure to read the *New York Times* Book Review and the Arts section on Sunday, as well as the *New Yorker* magazine and the *Atlantic Monthly*. A look at *Rolling Stone* and the *Village Voice* are important too. Following the work of certain great movie directors, painters, architects, and composers is a smart thing to do. They are all saying something worth listening to.

When Paul visited Athens and ended up at Mars Hill (see Acts 17), he addressed some of the city's better minds. Was he successful or not? The question has often been debated. I vote for success. I find his lecture spellbinding, a brilliant display of a great mind at work. It is all the evidence one needs that Paul was not a parochial man but a man of letters, in touch with his world, the literature, the thoughts of the best and worst of men.

It is no accident that this man could be comfortable in backwater towns like Derbe, business communities like Ephesus, political capitals like Rome, and intellectual centers like Athens. He knew how to talk with all people. And that was, in part, because he had the resilient man's quality of a disciplined mind.

TWENTY-TWO

RESILIENT PEOPLE HARNESS THEIR EMOTIONS

For many years Mike Singleterry played football for the Chicago Bears. He enjoyed a remarkable reputation both as a highly competitive athlete and as a devout Christian. One day, I was watching Singleterry and the Bears on television while they were losing a frustrating away game.

The hometown crowd behind the Bears' bench became ugly. They threw snowballs and shouted insults that no human being should have to hear. The TV cameras picked up the face of Singleterry as he turned and glowered at the people. He must have heard something specific from one of the spectators, because he suddenly lost his temper. He started toward the stands, shouting back. It was not Mike's finest hour.

But the hour *after* the game may have been one of Mike's finest, when he met with the press and apologized for his behavior. No excuses, no blaming: just an apology. His emotions had gotten out of control, he said, and he took responsibility for the bad moment.

Singleterry was dealing with something resilient people take seriously: the mastery, or the discipline, of emotions.

Several people in my past come to mind when I think of mastering (or not mastering) emotions.

The first was the one-time leader of a large Christian organization, who could raise enormous amounts of money but who had a streak of anger that could not be contained in moments of frustration. The second was a colleague, whose emotions could be described as mercurial. I never knew when I came to my office in the morning what this person's prevailing emotional expression would be: negative and critical or positive and lighthearted. And a third: a person who seemed to have no feelings whatsoever. There was an eerie sameness of response to every situation. We called him *steady,* but at the same time wondered if his life had any color at all.

I am not qualified to deal with the subject of emotions from a clinical perspective, but I know that most of us have an inner response mechanism that is not necessarily controlled by the logical or rational side of our brains. It reacts to people and events and, like a sudden storm, rises with strength from within, sometimes overwhelming us.

I used to pride myself on the fact that I kept my emotions to myself. I never saw myself as an angry person in that I did not use irate words, berate people, or lose my temper when there was a difficult moment. Then I got married, and my wife informed me that I had plenty of anger after all, and while it rarely came out in words, it showed itself in full color in facial expressions (the gift of glare, we called it) I never knew I had. I had work to do. I had emotions that needed to be disciplined.

Emotional reactions can surprise, even ambush us. We were watching the burial service of former president Ronald Regan, and as the bugler sounded the traditional "Taps," the TV camera closed in on the face of a Marine color guardsmen standing at attention.

His face was frozen in that typical military poise. But as the camera zoomed closer, it picked up the tears that were streaming down his cheeks. His emotions had begun to overcome the training.

Emotions must be disciplined, and resilient people work at this. They understand the tension that arises from possessing strong emotions that serve a worthy purpose, yet must never be permitted to rule one's choices or attitudes.

Among those biblical people who had problems with undisciplined emotions, there is Ahab. Take, for example, the day he came upon a vineyard owned by Naboth and sought to buy it. When Naboth informed him it was not for sale, Ahab lost control of himself:

> Ahab went home, sullen and angry because Naboth the Jezreelite had said, "I will not give you the inheritance of my fathers." He lay on his bed sulking and refused to eat. His wife Jezebel came in and asked him, "Why are you so sullen? Why won't you eat?" (1 Kings 21:4–5)

Ahab told her what had happened, and Jezebel responded, "Is this how you act as king over Israel? Get up and eat! Cheer up. I'll get you the vineyard of Naboth the Jezreelite" (v. 7).

Is there any difference between this conversation and one that an indulgent mother might have with a child throwing a temper tantrum? Naboth lost his life before this story was over, and Ahab got what he wanted.

As a boy, I was an emotional person. Tears came easily. Tears of fear if someone was harsh with me. Tears of empathy if I became aware of someone who was hurting badly. Tears in response to beautiful things: a story about love, a beautiful piece of music, something patriotic, an act of great courage.

But it often seemed that the people closest to me didn't understand or make room for such emotions. I am familiar with the words, "Stop crying, or I'll give you something to cry about." And I've heard, "Look at the crybaby" when involuntary tears came at the high point of a story. I became ashamed of those emotions and tried to mask them. I must not have been that successful if I couldn't even control a glare.

As a young pastor, I began to deny some of my emotions. It became less important for me to know how I was feeling and more important to deal with the emotions of others. Who was angry? Who was sad? Who was grieving? Who was exhilarated? When I found out the answers, I tried to offer the appropriate pastoral response. But my own emotions? I ignored them as much as possible.

I suspect that this failure to respect and then to discipline my emotions—to give them their due—led me toward some midlife difficulties that could have been avoided. How many times I had read (and preached on) God's question to Cain, "Why is your face downcast? Why are you angry?"! I hear God saying to Cain, "Listen to your emotion; listen to your feelings! They're sending you a message. Now do something about it!"

But if there were such messages when I was approaching my own Cain-like moment, I avoided them.

Resilient people are smarter than this. They discipline their emotions and make sure that they accurately reflect reality. They can be sad, joyful, angry, or elated in appropriate ways at appropriate times. Resilient people see their feelings as a significant part of the wholeness of life, but they do not allow them to become the final arbiter of conviction and choice. Yet, they are quite aware of them and take note if any one emotion begins to dominate life.

I think of Jesus in the Garden of Gethsemane in the hours before He was arrested and taken to the cross. His prevailing emotions seemed to be deep sadness and oppression. There's no indication of fear. The mysterious phrase that says He sweat drops of blood says something of the intensity of the hour. But He never lost His composure or His dignity. Other aspects of the being of Jesus are in control, and His commitment to do the will of His Father prevailed.

Some will remember the horrific video of the Korean who was kidnapped by Iraqi insurgents and was hours away from being beheaded. His emotions were in total charge, and he surrendered to panic and fear. "I do not want to die," he screamed to the camera.

Jesus, facing this same horror, acknowledged His dread of death: "Let this cup pass from me," He prayed (Matt. 26:39 KJV). But the dread did not rule His life or define His behavior.

What does it mean to discipline the emotions? Three thoughts have come to me in the last years. First, *I discipline my emotions when I make sure that they are not blocking the truths I need to hear.*

Some years ago I made a presentation to a group to whom I was accountable for leading an organization. I was asking authorization for something I wanted to do, and they said no. I did not respond well. I became silent, probably sullen, and for the rest of the evening I spoke only when spoken to. Even then my voice must have been edgy.

After the meeting, a friend steered me out the door and into a corner. His words, I shall not forget.

"You know, your behavior in there was not very classy. Those people were there to help you and to save you from making a bad mistake. But if they learn that you don't like hearing the word *no* on occasion, they'll stop telling you what they think, and you'll have to face the consequences all on your own."

My friend's rebuke prompted an examination of my own emotional reactions. He was right, and I knew it. What I learned that night has stuck with me for years and years. When I feel things going against me and feelings of anger or resentment begin to rise, it is time to stop and ask what is happening. Is this for the greater good or not? Is God speaking through this moment, or isn't He? I must not let my emotions mislead me.

Second, *I am disciplining my emotions when I make sure that they do not overrule what I know in my heart is good and right.*

In contrast to Jesus' remarkable composure on that awful night, Simon Peter lost his. After pledging complete fidelity to Jesus in the Upper Room (where it was safe), Peter lost his resolve in the servants' quarters of the home of the high priest of Jerusalem. Asked by a young girl if he knew Jesus, his courage failed, and he did the very opposite of his earlier promise: he betrayed the Lord.

Jesus, of course, had warned that this would happen. The Savior knew Peter better than he knew himself. He'd observed Peter's emotional ups and downs, and He knew that the pressures of the coming night would threaten Peter's emotional stability. The man's finest intentions would capitulate to fear.

A Simon Peter whose feelings were disciplined would have taken Jesus' warning seriously. He would have thought through, perhaps discussed with others, what the next hours might bring. What would be the correct behavior under such circumstances? How could the disciples support one another? What truths and convictions would one draw on if the pressure got too high?

Apparently, Peter learned all of this the hard way, because some time later he would stand before a formidable group of authorities, and, when told he could no longer preach in the streets, say, "We cannot help speaking about what we have seen and heard" (Acts 4:20). This is a new man!

Third, *I am disciplining my emotions when I take moments in a Sabbath to pause and ask, what are my prevailing feelings right now? Do they accurately reflect my situation? If I feel down, do I have reason to be down? If I am elated, does the reality of the moment justify that feeling? Is the anger I feel justified; is it in proportion to the situation?*

Israel's King Saul was a man who should have asked himself these questions. The jealousy in his heart toward young David began to destroy him. Slowly he became obsessed with getting rid of David.

You see him running throughout the wilderness, tracking David in hopes of killing him. And the more David alluded him, the more fixated he became. Nothing else counted.

It would have been a good time for Saul to stop and say to himself, *what's happening here that explains my conduct? Why am I allowing a mere kid to control my thinking?*

Finally, *I am disciplining my emotions if I am careful to translate them into responsible action.* If the feeling is an accurate reflection of the moment, we must act. Sometimes that means holding my emotions in check while I do what needs to be done. I see this happening on the deck of a doomed ship in a storm. Sailors and soldiers have all lost self-control in a supreme moment of terror. Then Paul stands up among them and says:

> "I urge you to keep up your courage, because not one of you will be lost . . . Last night an angel of the God whose I am and whom I serve stood beside me and said, 'Do not be afraid, Paul. You must stand trial before Caesar; and God has graciously given you the lives of all who sail with you.' So keep up your courage, men, for I have faith in God that it will happen just as he told me." (Acts 27:22–25)

Someone tells us that twenty-seven thousand children are dying every day in this world from preventable causes. The cost of saving those lives is almost negligible. Many people hearing this feel a pang of emotion: pity, disgust over the callousness of governments, horror that innocent children die prematurely. But a moment later the emotion is forgotten because we are on to something else that is brighter and happier. This is wasted emotion.

We are greatly perturbed because someone has mistreated another person, and we feel stirred enough to say, "Someone ought to do something about this." We are gripped by something said in a talk or a book that pertains to the way we are presently living, and we feel the strong emotional press to change. But an hour later the feeling is forgotten and nothing happens.

William Barclay wrote:

There is nothing more dangerous than a repeated experiencing of a fine emotion with no attempt to put it into action. It is a fact that every time a man feels a noble impulse without taking action, he becomes less likely ever to take action. In a sense it is true to say that a man has no right to feel sympathy unless he at least tries to put that sympathy into action. An emotion is not something in which to luxuriate; it is something which at the cost of effort and of toil, and of discipline and of sacrifice, must be turned into the stuff of life.[1]

As I wrote earlier, Gail and I spent several days at ground zero during the first week after the Trade Towers were hit by planes flown by terrorists. We were there each day from noon until well after midnight trying to meet some of the physical and spiritual needs of the police and firefighters who were in the first wave of rescuers. These were the days when it was still hoped that we could find people trapped in the rubble.

Those days at ground zero will probably rate as among the most emotionally draining days of my life. In the same moments we saw people totally lose control of their feelings and dissolve into inconsolable grief, and we saw others who disciplined their emotions and gathered strength for the horrible tasks they had to pursue.

I was at the west gate, where teams of men and women formed up to engage the smoking pile of debris that, a few days earlier, was the World Trade Center. Here was a circle of firefighters who were collecting their tools and their breathing apparatus.

"How long have you been here?" I asked.

"We've been here since right after the towers went down."

"That's four straight days," I said. "Don't you think you should at least take three or fours hours and crawl into a hole someplace and sleep?"

"We've got brothers in there, and they could still be alive. If they're there, we're going to find them. Until then we don't need no sleep."

"Then let me say a prayer for you." And as I concluded my prayer, I said, "And Lord God, help these men to remember that New York City loves them very much. And that You love them dearly."

When I finished praying, most of the men were sobbing. I held several of them in my arms in a masculine embrace and felt their bodies trembling with the grief and shock of what had happened. I felt their sweaty, unshaved cheeks against mine. We were all men out on the edge of emotions we'd never felt before.

Then, emotions retrieved, they lined up, slung their air tanks over their shoulders, picked up their shovels and their bottles of water, and headed into the rubble.

It's times like this that you find out how resilient you are. And whether or not your emotions are disciplined.

TWENTY-THREE

RESILIENT PEOPLE TRIM THEIR EGOS

———

The word *perp walk* has stolen into our vocabulary in just the last few years. It is shorthand for that humiliating moment when a person of wealth or power is handcuffed by the police and marched away to a court appearance in full view of the press.

Any of us who have known some kind of public humiliation can easily identify with the one in restraints. We know the feeling of mortification even if we cannot put it into words. Once you dared to think you were something or somebody. But a perp walk (or something similar to it) brings on the feeling of being nothing. Behind all of this is the ego.

The ego exists in the interior life. It is the centerpiece of the self, and it has an entrepreneurial passion to expand itself . . . even at the expense of others, if necessary. The Scripture reader believes that this ego is part of the creative handiwork of God in the making of humanity, but that the ego is affected by a spiritual virus (shall we say) ever since evil infected the world. From that point on the ego has been both a problem and an asset.

When something has the potential for good, you don't obliterate it. But if it also has potential for being destructive, it must be disciplined, kept *under control.* This is why those of us who walk in the Christian way think about the great grace of *humility.*

"Humility," wrote Archbishop William Temple, "does not mean thinking less of yourself than of other people, nor does it mean having a low opinion of your own gifts. *It means freedom from thinking about yourself at all*"[1] (emphasis mine).

Moses must have been keenly aware of the power of the ego. Perhaps because there were times in his life when he had to discipline his own so severely. What's behind the words, "Moses was a very humble man, more humble than anyone else on the face of the earth" (Num. 12:3)?

I think of his impulsive act in killing an Egyptian, apparently thinking that this would be a gesture of leadership that would win the respect of the Hebrew slaves and establish him as something of a savior. The action backfired, and Moses was soon fleeing the city as a fugitive. A self-induced perp walk (or run).

It took forty years of living like a shepherd (and how the Egyptians despised shepherds!) to discipline this man's ego. Only then—at the age of eighty—was he ready to live life on God's terms. The man that emerged from the desert was decidedly different from the man who entered it.

Perhaps I keep coming back to this episode in Moses' life because it reflects one of the great questions of the Bible—how do resilient people tame their egos and put them in submission to the purposes of God? Apparently the ego does not easily submit to regulation in most of us. It insists on having its own way and grabbing "space" and recognition it does not deserve.

The most profound expression of ego out of control is that attributed to Lucifer, the fallen angel:

You said in your heart, . . . "I will raise my throne above the stars of God; I will sit enthroned on the mount of assembly

. . . I will ascend above the tops of the clouds; I will make myself like the Most High." (Isa. 14:13–14)

And then Scripture says in response to this:

But you are brought down to the grave, to the depths of the pit. (v. 15)

A Babylonian king, Nebuchadnezzar, seems to have been in a similar mood when he walked on the roof of his palace, looked out over the city, and puffed, "Is not this the great Babylon I have built as the royal residence, by my mighty power and for the glory of my majesty?" (Dan. 4:30)

In both cases there was something like a perp walk. Both Lucifer and Nebuchadnezzar were humbled.

As I think about the nature of resilient people, it comes to me that one of the secrets of self-mastery is the deliberate discipline of this thing called the ego, which—left to itself—will betray and weaken us.

Some years ago, Gail and I had the opportunity to spend a week working on a Habitat for Humanity project in Hungary. Former president Jimmy Carter and his wife, Rosalyn, were assigned to the house being built right next to the one we were working on. It gave me a chance to glance over every once in a while to see what the former president was doing.

He never seemed to stop working. He arrived before anyone else, toured the ten homes that were being constructed, and arranged for subtle adjustments in the delivery of supplies so that no work crew on any of the ten homes got ahead of the others, creating an unnecessarily competitive climate. He made it clear to fellow construction workers that he was there to work and would not have time to visit with "rubbernecks." If people desired to take pictures, that, he said, would have to wait until the project was finished.

At mealtime we all gathered in a huge feeding tent. I noted that President Carter always took a place at the end of the line for the food table. He used the same portable bathrooms everyone else used. He stayed in the same housing that all of us endured. Throughout the week it was clear that he resisted any special privileges to which he might have been entitled.

In such ways I watched President Carter discipline his ego.

Resilient people understand that ego has an insatiable desire for enlargement. Left undisciplined, it becomes addicted to expansion. The interior side builds and builds a false view of self until there is *hubris,* a Greek term describing a person who is so full of himself that he loses all touch with reality. The exterior side adorns the ego with every symbol of glamour, power, and notoriety that can be acquired. We see it in the extremes of a tyrant that can never own enough palaces.

It is easy to rag on the so-called rich and famous. But the battle of ego creep is no less serious for those of us who think of ourselves as relatively simple and modest in our ways of life.

I live with the temptation to ego creep almost every day of my life. Perhaps it has known a bit of discipline after my own "perp walk" of almost twenty years ago. But it is nevertheless still there, and if I am not careful, it will surge back out of control in ways I never expected.

This is a most difficult chapter to write in this book. How illusory is the subject of ego and humility. How impossible it is to reduce the ideas to simple, foolproof formulas. And how fearsome it is to even hint that the challenge of the ego is ever fully met. We all know full well that the issue of the ego is likely to be one's greatest struggle until the end of life.

A search of Scripture will underscore the fact that God had to purify the egos of some of the Bible's most notorious men. Abraham, Joseph, Moses, David, Simon Peter, Paul: every one of them suffered in one way or another until their egos were reduced to true size.

"Nothing is like humility," wrote John Chrysostom. He went on using the strongest possible language:

> This is mother, and root and nurse and foundation and bond of all good things: without (humility) we are abominable and execrable and polluted.[2]

The aging person struggles with ego when he becomes indignant that a new generation is passing him by and cares little about what he has done or what he thinks. A midlife person does battle with ego each time he or she compares life with the ways others are living it. A young adult is dealing with ego when she assumes that nothing is good enough for her.

So what does it mean to discipline the ego?

I found that I must meditate each day on my brokenness in life and the redemptive work of Christ to mend it back together again. When Col. Samuel Logan Brengle of the Salvation Army was once introduced to an audience as the "great Colonel Brengle," he wrote in his journal:

> If I appear great in their eyes, the Lord is most gracious helping me to see how absolutely nothing I am without Him and helping keep me little in my own eyes. He does use me. But I am so conscious that *He* uses me, and that it's not of me that the work is done. The axe cannot boast of trees it has cut down. It could do nothing but for the woodsman. He made it, he sharpened it, he used it, and the moment he throws it aside it becomes only old used iron. Oh, that I may never lose sight of this.[3]

I have tried to learn the importance of seeking out the company of those people who are weak, who are struggling, who are poor. And what I do with them, I must be careful to keep secret. It should be done with no mind toward recognition or reward. If one is praised incessantly for his work on behalf of others, the ego expands again.

In the discipline of ego, Gail and I have endeavored to set reasonable limits on our lifestyle. These limits must be informed by our conscience and the work of God's Spirit. In the words of Amy Carmichael, "We do follow a crucified and stripped Savior," and it is a daily challenge to remain mindful of this so as not to become seduced by the notion that there are privileges and things we deserve which others do not have.

Albert Sweitzer was once asked why he traveled third class wherever he went. "Because there is no fourth class," he said. The ego is fed in dangerous ways when I take every liberty to elevate my lifestyle in materialistic ways that increasingly separate me from people of lesser means.

Who of us—in the dark places of our lives—does not want to be overly admired, respected, even envied? Left to our devices, we crave each bit of self-worth that can be built upon the applause and regard of people. Thus the temptation: give them something to admire you for.

And so we talk.

Ego is disciplined if I listen carefully to those who love me the most *and* to those who are my critics. Especially my critics whose words, I must assume, contain at least a kernel of truth from which I can learn.

There is a small core of friends, I suppose, who would be truthful if they can be sure we will not turn on them. But most of those we call our friends are not likely—using Paul's words—to speak the truth in love (see Ephesians 4:15). And so, sometimes it is left to our critics to help us tame our egos as they remind us, often in harsh terms, of our dark sides and our poor decisions.

It is said that a young man, freshly graduated from one of England's greatest universities, came to live in the community led by

Gandhi. Soon after his arrival he was assigned to clean latrines as his daily contribution to the community's life. He protested the assignment to Gandhi, saying, "Don't you see who I am? I have great things to do." Gandhi replied, "I know you can do great things; what I don't know is if you can do little things"[4]

In such a way his ego was disciplined. This is the pathway of resilience.

TWENTY-FOUR

RESILIENT PEOPLE OPEN THEIR HEARTS TO THE PRESENCE OF GOD

Occasionally I have written about my grandfather, Thomas MacDonald, among the godliest men I have ever known. In his aging years he had sunk into deep dementia, and he was unable to recognize anyone around him, including those with whom he'd spent his entire life and who faithfully came to see him.

The day of my last visit was unbearably hot and humid. But when I walked into my grandfather's un-air-conditioned room, he was quietly seated by his bed, dressed in a woolen suit and tie. He was looking out the window with a serene expression on his face. In his lap lay a large opened Bible.

"Granddad!" I greeted him.

"And who are you?" he asked.

"I'm your grandson, Gordon. What are you doing here in your suit and tie? It's too hot to be dressed like that."

"Oh," he said, "you always want to be prepared in case the

people here would like to read the Bible and have a season of prayer."

This was my grandfather. There was little, if anything, left of his life. But to these things he would always be true: his love for God, his reverence for the Bible, and his readiness to serve others.

Grandfather was crossing the finish line of life, and he was doing it with a kind of resilience. He was dying as he'd lived: faithful, sacrificial, and calm-spirited.

Grandfather had been an engineer for the New York Central Railroad at the time he heard what he believed to be a call from God to enter missionary service. He walked away from a promising career, and for forty years gave himself completely to Europe, leading a missionary enterprise that deployed hundreds of people to cities and towns that would later come under Communist control after World War II.

He was one of the most spiritually disciplined men I have ever known. And when life reached its end, the spiritual disciplines continued until the very last.

Sitting near him during that final visit, I could tell by the odors in the room that his physical body was in its final stages of deterioration. He could not think clearly; he could not get in and out of bed without help; he could not even feed himself. But deep inside of him, at the core of his life, there was something still very much alive—his love and devotion to God.

John Milton, going blind at the age of forty-four, wondered aloud in his sonnet *On His Blindness* if he had any further value to God? He wrote:

> Thousands, at his bidding speed,
> And post o'er Land and Ocean without rest;
> *They also serve who only stand and wait.* (Emphasis mine)

Grandfather had once been among those who sped "o'er land and ocean without rest," but now it was his to only stand and wait. And he did it with resilience.

A haunting memory sticks from years and years ago, when news came of a young husband in our congregation who was dead by an errant shot during a hunting trip. It was my lot as the family's pastor to rush to the home and sit with the family. As I drove away from my home, I found myself asking, "And what shall I give this family? My spiritual resources are dry. All I have is words, but my spirit seems empty." It was a most miserable moment, a scary one for a youthful pastor. And one of those times when I determined I would never again be caught with an empty soul when others needed spiritual resource.

I came to see that I owed my congregation a filled-up soul. They needed this far more from me than all the church programs and visions I could put before them. Whether they encountered me in the pulpit or on the streets of our community during the week, they needed to know that if (perish the thought) there was only one human being in their world who had some experience in the presence of God, I would be that man.

To me, spiritual discipline is relatively uncomplicated. It begins with time—usually early in the morning—when the day is quiet. I have come to love those moments, and often they can extend to an hour or two. It is not that every morning is a rapturous experience, but the collective of the mornings, day after day, builds the spirit and makes of it a dwelling place for the Lord.

I try to rise early and seek God's heart. And how is such time used? I *worship* and, occasionally, write prayers of praise and exaltation. I *read* (Scripture and meditative literature). I *pray*. I *give thanksgiving*. I *reflect* on the events of the previous day and, finally, I try to *focus* on what I think God is saying about the use of today's hours and write down my intentions.

Worship: A day really should begin with a quiet recitation of God's great attributes and acts in history. One's day is best begun with the use of glorious words like *holy, love, steadfastness, grace, majesty, righteous, everlasting,* and *redeeming.* And each day should begin with thoughts of the acts of God: creating, transforming, delivering, sending, promising, inspiring, coming.

I love the liturgical worship that is provided through *The Book of Common Prayer* and other volumes that offer me the words of worship used by Christ-followers of other times. There are certain hymns to which I return again (showing my generation): "Great Is Thy Faithfulness," "O Love That Will Not Let Me Go," "When Morning Guilds the Skies," "Guide Me, O Thou Great Jehovah," "Crown Him with Many Crowns," and "It Is Well with My Soul."

———

My *reading* is first from the Scriptures and then from great classics of the Christian tradition. Augustine's confessions, Thomas a Kempis's *Imitation,* Fenelon's letters, Catherine Booth's letters, and A. W. Tozer's books are all soul-food for me.

Repeatedly I have returned to Bunyan's *Pilgrim's Progress,* and I take delight in attempting my own private modern-language translation of his Old English. Alexander Whyte's *Bunyan's Characters* has been a pleasant guidebook when I walk the path with Bunyan's Christian. I have loved including in my devotional times the great Christian biographies that tell the stories of great men and women who have suffered for the faith and shown themselves to be resilient people.

Not long ago I read through the biography of the great Anglican bishop Handley Moule and took note of comments he made about his father.

"I can only look back upon him," Moule says,

thankful that such a personality embodies to me the great word Father; a man so full of energy and capacity, so absolutely simple, so entirely fearless, so free from the seeking of his own glory, so ready both to bear and do, a gentleman so true, a Christian so strong, so spiritual, so deep, such a pastor, such a parent, such a grandfather, such a friend.[1]

On the day I read that paragraph, I copied it into my journal, because I found the words so inspirational as marks of a man or woman of God.

———

Praying! A challenge for an active, wandering mind like mine. I have learned to pray the Psalms, repeat the great prayers of the biblical saints, mouth the prayers of the *Book of Common Prayer*, and muse on the prayers of people like John Bailee. I am not an original or creative pray-er, and the prayers of others are quite helpful in assuring that I enlarge the range of my prayers.

"Lord, do you mind if I shout at you out of my heart?" I recently prayed. I found myself angry, boiling at the news that streams from Africa of dying and orphaned children, raped women, homeless refugees, millions of women with AIDS, villages with poisoned water. Does this kind of thing not call for a shout of anger, of anguish for the suffering of the world?

There are prayers for my family, my friends, for the church around the world. Prayers again for injustice and poverty. Prayers for the spiritually lost and wandering. Prayers for myself: of confession, the need for courage, for wisdom . . . much, much wisdom. There is the genuine ache of my heart to be a deeper person, one who reflects more of the character of Christ. It doesn't come fast enough, and that demands prayer.

———

Thanksgiving: for a remarkable wife; for children who love me and want me around; for close personal friendships; for people who are willing to listen to me preach and read my books; for strength, health, discernment. For opportunities which are mine to enter peoples' lives and offer encouragement and hope. For all the good things that happen during each day and for the lessons of wisdom that they yield.

———

Reflection. A word that describes the quiet moments when one asks what things mean. What happened yesterday, and what does it teach me? Where were things said for which I must repent? Where was time misused? Were there choices poorly made? And what were the blessings? Where did God answer prayer, show Himself in surprising ways, offer warnings that need to be heeded? What human needs did I ignore? And what is God's call for today?

Brother Lawrence said:

> We must examine with care . . . what are the virtues of which we stand most in need, what are those which are most difficult to win, the sins to which we most often fall, and the most frequent and inevitable occasions of our falling. We must turn to God in complete confidence in the hour of battle, abide strongly in the presence of his divine majesty, worship him humbly, and set before him our woes and weaknesses. And thus we shall find in him all virtues though we may lack them all.[2]

———

Focusing. Where is God leading today? What are the priorities that need to be addressed. Who needs my attention? What do I have to learn? Where might be the *landmines* in the day's journey? What needs to change?

In asking these questions, I hope to tune my soul to the voice of God so that I will be conscious of His guidance throughout the day. With increasing frequency this actually happens.

W. E. Sangster was doing this sort of reflection when he wrote in his journal:

> I believe that God has been knocking loudly on the door of my heart of late. I believe it for these reasons:
> a. I have lost peace: thoughts of great unrest and personal uncertainty have invaded my heart.
> b. I have lost joy: great depressions sweep over me and life seems a burden.
> c. I have lost taste for my work. I have had to lash myself to it instead of going willingly and gladly.
> d. Despite encouragements of one sort and another, I feel a failure.[3]

Such personal frankness, put on paper, helped Sangster to see where he needed to get back on track. Now he knew what to pray for; he understood what had to be changed.

Should I live to be 200, I doubt that I should ever have the gentle, godly demeanor of my grandfather, Thomas. But I know what a resilient man of spiritual discipline looks like, and I am determined to follow in his path. It will be at a distance, but I shall still follow.

V.

RESILIENT PEOPLE RUN IN THE COMPANY OF A "HAPPY FEW"

They learn the value of lingering.

They avoid the peril of the solitary life.

They know how friendship works.

They seek a "certain kind" of people.

THE "HAPPY FEW"

"We few, we happy few, we band of brothers"
—Shakespeare, *The Life of King Henry V*

It was a brilliant Saturday morning in late May. In a few days my senior class would be graduating from Stony Brook, and I would leave the school, the dirt track, and the white bulletin board and head home to Colorado and, eventually, to the University of Colorado in Boulder.

But all of that was relatively unimportant compared to the fact that this was the day when the eight teams in our prep-school league would meet to compete for the annual track and field championship. I was entered in three events: the 400 and 800 meters and the anchor leg in a final (always exciting) 800-meter relay race.

But for three of us there was a highly anticipated add-on to the day. When the track meet was over, two other team members and I would break away and join girlfriends for a dinner date and a movie. Permission for this had been requested from the school and granted. The understanding was that we would take the 10:30 PM Long Island Railroad train from the Huntington station back to the campus. This would assure our reaching the Stony Brook campus by the midnight curfew.

Curfews were serious business at Stony Brook. Weeks before, it had been made clear to seniors that the curfew rule would be enforced even on the last few weekends before graduation. A violation could result in suspension, which could mean a delay in graduation and the loss of the privilege of marching in the commencement procession. Imagine a disaster like that if your parents were driving two thousand miles in anticipation of seeing their son receive a diploma.

The plans the three of us had made for the evening were the talk of the team as we boarded the bus en route to the track meet. We were kidded unmercifully, and no one led the charge more vigorously than Coach Goldberg. "Now, Gordie," he'd said with a grin, "I'm worried about you becoming so starry-eyed over that beautiful girl that you'll miss the train. I don't want you calling me long after I'm in bed and saying, 'Sir, we're stranded in Huntington; would you come and get us?'"

"Sir," I assured him, "you have nothing to worry about. We've got a perfect plan for the evening. We'll actually be back in the dorm ahead of time. You'll have a great night's sleep."

Stony Brook won the league championship that day, and I walked off the track with the satisfaction that I had contributed to the team victory. As we joined our girlfriends and waved good-bye to the team, MWG called out once more from the door of the team bus, "Remember . . . no phone calls tonight."

The dinner went perfectly. The movie was terrific. Then came the last part of our arrangements. We would meet the father of one of the girls, who would take them home while we made our way to the train at the Huntington station a few blocks away. That was the plan, and it seemed foolproof.

But it didn't take into account the possibility that the father would be twenty minutes late and that we would feel compelled to remain with the girls until he arrived. When he did, we sprinted for the station. Unfortunately, when we arrived, we saw the red lights on the back of the train to Stony Brook disappearing down the track. For the first time in several years, a Long Island Railroad train had come and left the Huntington station on time.

Given our severely limited financial resources, a taxi was out of the question. And given our youthful male pride, we were not going to call any of the girls or their fathers.

"Who can we call to come and get us at this time of night?" became the operational question. The two or three people that came to mind weren't answering their phones at the eleven o'clock hour. Calling the school's main number seemed foolish since it would only verify our dilemma and, most likely, guarantee the graduation-delaying suspension we feared the most.

"We could call Goldberg," someone quietly suggested. Now the memories of his earlier remarks on the bus came back to haunt us.

"No, we can't call him. He'd think we'd planned it this way all along."

Minutes passed. It was now 11:15. Stony Brook was an hour away. It seemed as if the whole world was refusing to answer their telephones.

Then finally, "We've got to call him. Gordie, you're good at this sort of thing."

Reluctantly, shaking perhaps, I made the call. It was clear when he answered that the coach and his wife, Dorothy, were already asleep. I explained our dilemma.

"Gordie, are you being absolutely truthful with me? You boys didn't miss the train on purpose?" MWG asked.

"Sir, I'm telling you the absolute truth. We wouldn't ever want to do this to you."

"I'll be there in an hour. Now, Gordie, stay right where you are."

An hour later the Goldbergs drove up in front of the now-closed railroad station and picked up three very nervous teenage boys who knew they were in serious violation of the curfew rules. Forgotten were the glorious hours on the track; forgotten were the girlfriends. All pride and cockiness melted away.

Each of us wondered how the coach would handle this moment? Would he be angry? Would the ride back to the campus be filled with reprimands about our irresponsibility and how we had cost the Goldbergs the better part of a night's sleep? And would we be reminded about the penalties that awaited us back at the campus for violating curfew?

If this was our expectation, we could not have been more wrong.

The ride home was filled with laughter, with recollections of the day at the track, with conversation that put the three of us at ease and helped us restore our sense of dignity.

As we drove on to the campus, MWG finally said, "Now, gentlemen, you realize, of course, that there will be some difficult conversations about this on Monday. I don't know what may transpire, but I'll assure the headmaster that you didn't intend for the night to end this way."

What did happen on Monday? My memory is a bit foggy. Something gracious must have occurred, because I did graduate (on schedule), and soon after I was headed back to Colorado.

"Gordie, from now on you can call me Marvin," MWG had said soon after graduation ceremonies were over. It was a symbol of the fact that I was no longer his student and runner but that I was now his friend. When we had first met, he had changed my name. And now that I was leaving, he was changing the way I would address him.

Of that unforgettable Saturday night, I have these memories: Marvin Goldberg taught me one more thing about the elements of resilience. The subject: *the importance of personal relationship*. Unlike other lessons, this one was not learned on the track, but in the late-night hours, when three of his protégés were stranded and rather desperate. The coach gave us one last tutorial, this time about the meanings of friendship and grace. Just as he had asked me, three years before, to trust him, he had now chosen to trust me and my explanation of our predicament. And he'd left the comforts of his bed and home to come where we were.

Now, it was not, "Gordie, come here please"; rather, it was the reverse. It was me calling out, "Sir, come and get me, please." And he had. Can you imagine what this meant—to be treated with such dignity—when one is barely across the line of an eighteenth birthday?

Over a lifetime I have had the opportunity to respond to calls from friends that were not dissimilar to the one I made to MWG that night. I have heard more than a few versions of "Come and get me, please." Occasionally, the calls have been on the desperate side, and the cost of responding was significant. If I have been tempted to beg off or to find reasons why this might not be a convenient moment, my mind has snapped back to that crazy night when, as a teenage boy, I found myself in trouble and the coach came and rescued me.

The older we get, the more we come to understand the inestimable value of the "happy few," that inner circle of intimate friends who will always be there long after the lights of the fast and glamorous life have been extinguished. The "happy few" may be the most important treasure one will ever possess this side of heaven. Resilient people know this from experience.

THE VALUE OF LINGERING

He appointed twelve . . . that they might be with him.
—MARK 3:14

Our daughter, Kristy, and her family live close by, and occasionally she and I arrange to have an early-morning breakfast together at the local Egg Shell Restaurant. Today was one of those occasions.

Once seated and having placed our order, we began to talk about last Friday night, when a few dozen people in our small town of Canterbury gathered in a backyard to celebrate a tenth wedding anniversary. It was not what you'd call a church group, although many of the people in the group are a part of one kind of church or another. No, the makeup of the group was just . . . well, friends, neighbors, folks with whom we all share life.

Many of the women in the group participate in a food-purchasing co-op. Each has some sort of skill, and they often meet to help each other make things. Those who have preschool children gather on Thursday mornings so their kids can play together. The men hang out somewhat regularly to talk about "guy things." They're always sharing tools, helping one another complete projects, or, in the winter, plowing snow. You get the feeling when you're with this group, as we were on Friday, that everyone genuinely likes one another.

Over time, many in the group have begun to gather to read the Bible and discuss the implications. Sometimes they agree to read a particular book and chat about it. As a result, more than a few have slowly, almost imperceptibly, crossed the line into personal Christian faith.

When you've been a pastor all your life, most gatherings of people mean serious conversations about problems and programs. You feel responsible to make sure every encounter has a purpose, and when such events end, you go home assessing what's been accomplished. It's work. A virtuous work, I hope. But work, nevertheless.

Friday night's gathering seemed different. No work. No stress, no hassle, no worrying about everybody's happiness. Just forty people (adults and children) hanging out under a New England starry sky, arranging and rearranging themselves in order to play or talk. Forty people making sure that two friends celebrating a tenth anniversary knew that they were loved and admired.

"What's the secret behind such a laid-back fellowship?" I asked Kristy this morning.

"Lingering," she said, choosing a word I'd never heard her use before. "No one is in a hurry. There's no pressure to make something happen. People are not burdened by expectations of dress, correctness of opinion, or responsibilities for various programs. They just like being together. They really care about each other. No one is in a hurry to get somewhere else. They just . . . linger."

Lingering! An interesting word. I asked Kristy what the word meant to her.

"Dad, when the women meet at my house for Bible study, they come in their pajamas [you can do this in a rural community]. You know that you've reached a level of real openness when you can do that. And the guys . . . when they meet, they like to tell their stories and allow serious topics to arise out of the flow of conversation. They learn lots from each other. It begins with everyone assuming that everyone has something to offer. So, lingering means that we hang out."

Kristy is describing something that I wish I saw more of in the organized church. What she describes feels right. A collection of people who think it's all right just to linger without always having to measure things in terms of results.

Twenty years ago, when I was forced to assess the direction and quality of my life-journey, I concluded that one of the areas in need of an overhaul was my view of personal relationships. Up until that time I had done poorly in the area of what Kristy calls *lingering* friendships; they just weren't part of my life's job description.

As I looked critically at myself, I began to realize that I was a poor friend to those whom I called friends. And, truth be told, if any of them were trying to extend lingering friendship to me, I probably was unaware. I was too involved in my work; I was probably self-absorbed; and I didn't fully comprehend what the Bible taught concerning the sacredness of *human connection*. I believed those who said that the cost of leading meant loneliness and few friends.

If I had remained like that, I don't think there would be much resilience in my life today.

During that time of midlife assessment, Gail and I came to an uncomfortable conclusion about our own relationship. While we loved each other and believed our marriage to be sound and enduring, the fact was that it lacked something. We came to see that, when our children left home, we allowed our lives to become too serious, too much defined by our work. We liked most of the things we were doing, but the fact was that there was less laughter, less play, and less time to . . . linger with each other or friends. This blind spot had cost us dearly.

Further examination convinced us that most of the relationships we did have were based on who had problems and needed fixing, who was staffing or leading the programs at church, or who was on the program at some conference where one or both of us was speaking.

We concluded that this was not a healthy way to live, and if we didn't change, there would be undesirable consequences as we pointed toward the second half of life with all of its vulnerabilities.

Recognizing this, we set out to build some of what Kristy identifies as lingering friendships.

Over the years I have come to call this special group of people the "happy few," a phrase lifted from Shakespeare's *The Life of King Henry V.* In his attempt to rally his beleaguered English troops, who would face the French in the battle of Agincourt, Henry spoke of a "band of brothers . . . *we few, we happy few*" (emphasis mine).

> And gentlemen in England now abed
> Shall think themselves accursed they were not here,
> And hold their manhood cheap while any speaks
> Who fought with us on St. Crispian's day.

In thinking through what a happy few might look like, I saw the need for some close male friendships. And Gail and I recognized a further need to bond together with some married couples on a regular basis.

Let me emphasize that we did not have in mind tea circles or supper clubs. We came to believe in the importance of something like an extended family where there would be a deep commitment to meet with one another regularly, to share life and its challenges, and to help each other find out what God was saying to us.

The resilient life—this long-distance race—is not possible without such a personal community. One cannot meet all the needs there are for deep human intimacy within the confines of a marriage alone.

There must be others with whom the journey is shared. In fact, if we ask a marriage to provide all of our needs for human intimacy, the marriage may droop under the weight of excessive demands.

In my youth we sang a popular chorus in church that helps me partly understand why it took so long for me to figure some of this out:

> If you know the Lord, *you need nobody else*
> To see you through the darkest night.
> *You can walk alone*, you need nobody else
> To keep you on the road marked right[1] (Emphasis mine)

The purpose of the song, of course, was to highlight the priority of one's commitment to Jesus, but it did so at the expense of an important truth: *we do need somebody else.* In fact, it may actually be the "somebody else" that Jesus uses to see us through the darkest night or to keep us on the road marked right. In most cases Jesus does this sort of thing through the very people the song implies we do not need.

Who are the happy few in our lives? Brace yourself for the answer we came up with: *the happy few are ultimately defined as the people we want to die with.*

All of us connect with people with whom we work, people with whom we live in our neighborhoods, and people with whom we serve and worship in our churches. But these tend to be connections that are like the waves of an ocean: they rise, foam for a moment, and then are gone. With the dramatic increase in the pace of life, most relationships are short-lived. But in the midst of all of this wildness, there must be a happy few who walk with one another, as it were, all the way to the grave.

Scholars suggest that most of us are capable of knowing about 150 people. In a book called *The Tipping Point,* author Malcolm Gladwell says, "The figure of 150 seems to represent the maximum number of individuals with whom we can have a genuinely social relationship, the kind of relationship that goes with knowing who they are and how they relate to us."[2]

Putting it another way, it's the number of people you would not feel embarrassed about joining uninvited for a drink if you happened to bump into them in a Starbucks.

But then Gladwell identifies another group within the group of 150, a *sympathy group*. He suggests that this group will number between 10 and 15 people. "Make a list," he writes, "of all the people you know whose death would leave you truly devastated."

There we are: the folks who would be at graveside, not as spectators, but as *deeply involved mourners* if something happened to us. And they are the folks at whose grave we would be present if something happened to them.

When I harshly critiqued myself twenty years ago on the paucity of my personal friendships, I imagined my own funeral and who might come. I suspected that there might be a modest crowd, but I had a hard time identifying those who might qualify as the *deeply involved mourners*. These would be those with whom I had lingered, and I hadn't done much lingering up until that point in my life. As the song put it, "I need[ed] nobody else."

So Gail and I set out to build a community of those who might fit the description of the happy few. Of course, I would hope that if and when that dramatic graveside moment comes, they might be *the unhappy few* for at least a few minutes.

Life together with a happy few begins with a biblical principle: that God does much of His work in our lives through personal relationships.

"A new command I give you," Jesus said to His disciples just before He went to the cross. "Love one another. As I have loved you, so you must love one another. By this all men will know that you are my disciples, if you love one another" (John 13:34–35).

Twenty years ago, when I pondered this statement with the fresh eyes of one whose life needed rebuilding, I began to see how much I had misjudged the intent of our Lord.

He had not loved these men simply by calling them into meetings so as to organize an institution. Rather, He had engaged them with a challenge, "follow Me," and promised them that change and growth would be part of the bargain. As one gospel writer put it, He invited them "to be with Him." Sounds like lingering to me.

Jesus opened up His life in a most practical way by living with the Twelve, traveling with them, sharing the harshness of life with them. He spoke truth into their lives even when it meant inflicting pain. He taught them by example how to pray, how to enter the lives of people, how to make decisions about when to respect tradition and when to break with it. He gave them leadership skills and relational skills. And then He set them free through His power to respond to a call and grow into their potential.

But there was something beyond all of this training and preparation for apostolic life. The Lord called them to become a happy few, a band of brothers, and at the beginning of the process, that might have seemed a total absurdity. After all, the group probably began as an unhappy few.

How might Matthew, a tax collector, get along with Simon the Zealot when, previously, they would have been pleased to kill one another over the contrast in their politics? How might an impulsive Simon Peter team up with a melancholy, doubting Thomas? I tell you that the fact that these disparate men became a band of brothers, a happy few, is no less a miracle than when Jesus raised the dead.

———

Jesus made it happen by lingering with His disciples in ways Kristy was describing to me just this morning. When she and I left the Egg Shell Restaurant and began our morning routines—she mothering her children, I writing this book—I had a lot to think about. Do you want to be a resilient person, and better, one who nurtures the resiliency of your "happy few"? Then learn a lesson from my daughter: Learn the lesson of lingering.

TWENTY-SIX

THE PERIL OF
THE SOLITARY LIFE

Among my most enjoyable activities is my participation in conferences around the world, where men and women in Christian leadership gather for a few days of spiritual refreshment. I like to start the first presentation by saying, "I'm not here to urge you to make your church bigger, or to talk about casting a larger vision, or why you should launch another program. That's for others to do. I'm here just to talk about *you* and the state of your soul."

It may be my imagination, but when I say this, I sense a feeling of relief sweep through the audience. The speaker has urged the listener to forget about all the busy stuff and simply concentrate on his or her own spiritual well-being for a few hours. Leaders don't get to do that very often.

Talking about the state of one's soul doesn't go very far before the subject of one's "happy few" comes on the table. Who are the people who populate that inner circle that, presumably, will walk through life with each of us and who will make an inestimable contribution to the development of our resilient life?

Raise that subject, and you get a lot of attention. For many there is no happy few. Henri Nouwen was thinking about this when he said, "Most Christian leadership is exercised by people who do not know how to develop healthy, intimate relationships and have opted for power and control instead. Many Christian empire-builders have been people unable to give and receive love."[1]

I am aware that more than a few people who read this chapter will not consider themselves "Christian leaders," but I ask them not to exempt themselves from the possibility that Nouwen's comment could apply nonetheless.

At the conferences I've mentioned, there are times for questions and discussion. If I were to identify the topic most frequently addressed, it would probably be the issue of personal relationships. The questions sound like this: "Where do you find friends?" "How do you make and maintain a close friendship?" "What do you do with your friends?" "Where do you get the time?"

From where I see things, the issue of a happy few in one's life is right at the top of the thinking of Christian men and women when you ask about the state of the soul. And it becomes an increasingly important issue as one gets older. Somehow the thought of the second half of life without a happy few is disheartening.

When I talk privately with people, I begin to hear some common themes. The first of these themes is really a theological issue. The faith taught to so many of us is a faith of individualism. It centers heavily on the transaction between Jesus and me. It rarely focuses on the idea of Jesus and *us*. Remember the song in the previous chapter.

It has been pointed out to me more than once that Jesus never seems to have a one-on-one conversation with any of His disciples. Even those that seem to be personal are always done in the company of others who were in a position to listen and form their own conclusions.

It was some of my Asian Christian friends who began to convince me that there was an entirely different way to understand the Bible:

through the lens of *community,* God doing His work in our lives through one another. In other words, I cannot grow into what God wants me to be (and do) unless I am in tight formation with some others.

When I talk with those who have no happy few, I often hear that they are too busy to take the time to develop relationships. They have great intentions; they do not even debate the necessity of the happy few. But building relationships is time-intensive, and they have convinced themselves that the time is simply not there.

For many years I moved among some of the most delightful people I could ever want to meet. Sometimes they were preachers and organizational leaders, but for the most part they were Christian people who were involved in interesting professions and pursuits of life. Time and again I would say to them, "We've got to get together sometime."

If Gail overheard me, she would say later, "I listened to you tell that man that you'd like to get together with him. He's probably going home tonight saying to himself, 'Gordon wants to get together.' He may be telling his wife right now what you said. And he'll be looking forward to your call. But you know what? He's not going to get a call, because you're too busy. I know you meant what you said at the moment, but by tomorrow you will have gotten on to other things, and your promise will be forgotten."

More than once I protested when Gail would say this. I had every intention in the moment to do what I promised. But the painful reality was that she was right. I didn't do what I said I was going to do. In a sense I was lying to them and lying to myself. My intention to get together was just that: an intention, a noble desire. But I was too busy; life moved too fast.

I began to see that busyness is a condition that we ourselves create. And when the day came that I realized that the resilient life was heavily dependent upon my connection with a happy few, I moved my friends toward the top of the priority list. Admittedly, I have a wife who has helped make this happen by maintaining the family calendar and making sure that friends get into the prime-time-blocks several weeks—sometimes months—before anything else creeps into the schedule.

I've noted that some of us miss out on life in the company of a happy few because we choose to spend the bulk of our time with people who need fixing and rescuing. We like the prominence of being the strong person in the group, who solves problems, answers questions, gives advice, and calls the shots. Everyone else just falls into line.

This is not atypical in Christian circles, where unraveling people's difficulties seems to be a high priority. We are tempted to think that a conversation is not substantial if it doesn't have something to do with repairing someone's broken life or rebuilding his or her priorities.

This is a simple trap to fall into, and it makes one feel superior and significant. I know. I feel as if I lived this way for any number of years in my early adulthood. And I assumed that this was the way God's work was done. It felt good to drive home at the end of an evening and say to Gail, "Well, it's been a wonderful night of ministry."

I'm thinking of a woman who gave herself to helping countless numbers of women through all their personal crises and questions. Almost all of her relationships, she realized later, tended (although inadvertently) to be one-way associations: one person always helping, counseling, consoling others. But none of these relationships were built on a true sense of reciprocity. Then she experienced a family crisis herself.

In that moment a most revealing thing occurred. Almost no one—all these women she had helped—called to inquire about *her* welfare. No one called to see how she was doing. No one *seemed* to care enough to find out. And it became a terrible disillusionment. The reasonable question: Who is there for me after I've tried so hard to be there for others?

Later, the explanations came. "I can't imagine you having a problem that you can't handle," someone said. "I didn't have the slightest idea what to say to someone like you," another commented. "You always seem so strong," from a third. "I guess we all figured you could take care of everything without us." And, "I didn't want to embarrass you."

It is obvious why one might want to avoid being part of a happy few if there is a strong, maybe even unconscious, fear of revealing one's secrets. The man or woman who cannot afford to show weakness, who has a need to be right, or always has to have things under personal control will likely have few, if any, intimates.

On a couple of occasions I have alluded to the moment when Jesus went to the Garden of Gethsemane with His disciples. "Could you men not keep watch with me for one hour?" He asks Peter (Matt. 26:40). I hear Jesus expressing a vulnerability that might be uncomfortable for the person who always has to appear strong. The Savior is admitting that He needs friends. And they're letting Him down.

Building the company of a happy few will probably not be attractive to someone who is resistant to being challenged about the way he lives or the way he thinks or the way he walks with God. Allow a few friendships to grow, and you begin to hear some rebukes, some corrections, some warnings. It's much easier to walk through life rendering opinions and judgments; much harder to listen and learn.

In my life as a pastor, I have met any number of people who have built walls about themselves, a wall of humor (let's say), or a wall of strong political or doctrinal opinion, or a wall of unmatchable competence. They keep this wall high so that no one ever gets near to the real person behind the walls. They are untouchable at soul level.

But if, for whatever reason, you get inside those walls, you are likely to discover tremendous insecurity. Challenge such a person and you are likely to be met with anger, or cries of hurt and offense, or withdrawal. This is a person who cannot stand for anyone to threaten the structure of his or her world, and it is easier to remain aloof and lonely than to enter into the give-and-take that comes when relationships are supple and solid.

There is one more reason why people sometimes resist the company of a happy few, and it could be the most significant, the reason behind all the other reasons.

Many of us fear being hurt, betrayed, turned against [you pick] . . . *again.* This is the person who at one time had great hopes of the intimacy that comes from a close marriage and close friends. But something terrible happened. The relationships deteriorated or imploded. The loss was grievous. And it leaves in its wake a determination that one would never risk opening up life again with anyone else. A shade is pulled over the heart just as one pulls a shade down to close off a window.

Basil Pennington wrote:

> We are broken persons and live in broken communities in a state of brokenness. We are alienated from ourselves and from each other. We do not readily fit together. We are like a bunch of porcupines trying to huddle together for warmth, who are always driven apart out of fear of the wound we can inflict upon each other with our quills.[2]

A movie celebrity announces to the press, "I'll never marry again." She says this after her second divorce, each the result of a partner's infidelity. "I'll never trust a friendship with someone in ministry again," another says when there is a harsh division between them. "The risk of getting close is just too great."

One wonders if Jesus ever felt hurt when His closest friends, the disciples, deserted Him. And one asks what's behind Paul's comment when, in a wistful moment, he writes to Timothy, "No one came to my support, but everyone deserted me" (2 Tim. 4:16).

Pain and disappointment are part of the risk in relationships.

For after all, we are, as Pennington wrote, "broken persons and [living] in broken communities in a state of brokenness."

If God continually reaches out for the hand of unfaithful people such as all of us, and if He does it because He wants to establish an intimate relationship, isn't something of significance being said? Aren't we hearing that one simply cannot stop trying in this business of seeking out friendship with a happy few? That we must try, and try, and try again?

Living resiliently cannot be done alone.

TWENTY-SEVEN

HOW FRIENDSHIP WORKS

———

A man I hold in high esteem and I were engaged in a discussion about things where there was some disagreement. At one point in the conversation he said, "Gordon, there's a root of bitterness in you."

The words stung. There is in parts of my family line something of a pattern of bitterness, and I have striven all of my life to make sure that this was not a part of my character. So when this man— whose opinion I have always respected—said, "There's a root of bitterness in you," I was stopped in my tracks.

"I'll think about that very carefully," I remember saying.

And I did. I gathered with three friends whom I would include among the happy few in my world. I told them about the remark, and then added, "I would like it if you would take the next week or two and think about this. If you want to get together and talk about me behind my back, that's OK. But I need to know this: Have you heard anything in my conversation or sensed anything in my conduct that might hint of bitterness or anger? I really need to know."

A week after this exchange, the three got together with me. "Gordon," one of them said, "we've given your question a lot of thought, and we've discussed it. We want you to know that we've seen nothing of the sort in you. The man was wrong."

The importance of this conversation to me cannot be overstated. Left to myself, I would have simply assumed that my critic was correct. I would have spent lots of energy trying to explore by myself what might not have been there. But my friends freed me from a futile exercise. This is one of the fruits of being part of a happy few. And it's what resilient people seek.

"I love to view all my Christian friends as fuel," said Charles Simeon, my nineteenth-century hero, as he spoke to a group of pastors. "Having gathered you all together at my hearth, I warm myself at your fire, and find my Christian love burn and grow."

A careful study of the Bible will lead one to realize something many of us were not adequately taught when we were young: that the Bible is about relationships and that no one is a complete human being apart from the context of those relationships. It is the truly Christian perspective.

Jesus Himself understood that the apex of His suffering on the cross had less to do with physical pain and more to do with aloneness. "Father, why have You forsaken me?" He screamed out. Isolation is the epitome of hell.

In Nelson Mandela's autobiography, *Long Walk to Freedom*, he describes life on Robben Island where he and other political prisoners spent almost thirty years. He reminisces on the relationships that tightened during those years of intense suffering.

The authorities' greatest mistake was to keep us together, for together our determination was reinforced. We supported each other and gained strength from each other. Whatever we knew, whatever we learned, we shared, and by sharing we multiplied whatever courage we had individually. That is not to say that we were all alike in our responses to the hardships we suffered. Men have different capacities and react differently to stress. But the stronger ones raised up the weaker ones, and both became stronger in the process.[1]

This is the resilient life from the perspective of one who has realized that you cannot make it through a lifetime without the company of a happy few.

We've taken a quick look at why some avoid such connections. But I believe it would be even more beneficial if we asked ourselves, why is it important to embrace such connections?

I have become convinced, for example, that in the company of a happy few, we are much more likely to hear God speak the truth we need to hear. A group of godly men were together at the moment when the Holy Spirit spoke and called Saul and Barnabas to a ground-breaking mission of carrying the Christian gospel to Gentile nations. "While they were worshiping the Lord and fasting, the Holy Spirit said . . ." (Acts 13:2).

It is said that when Saint Francis sought God's will as to whether he should go into the world and serve the poor or retreat from the world to pray for the poor, he called his closest friends to him and asked that they might pray for an extended time on his behalf.

Then, at an appropriate moment many weeks later, he recalled them, washed their feet, prepared them a meal, and gave them fresh clothes. When they were sufficiently refreshed, he knelt before them and asked this question: "What does my Lord Jesus command from me?"

With such a question he asserted his conviction that God would speak through the happy few in his life. "He commands that you should go to the poor," was their answer. And he obeyed.

Resilient people also discover that, in close union with friends, they gain a sharper focus on the realities of life around them. I have come to see that my perspectives on things happening are just that . . .

perspectives. Often my perceptions of what someone has said or done, what is truly important in the world, what is the best response to a situation, are woefully inadequate until I have listened to others whom I trust. Only then do I stand on firmer ground about what is "truly true."

An African proverb warns about trying to walk through life forming opinions and judgments without the benefit of friends:

Alone I have seen many wonderful things, none of which are true.

As a man, I have come to appreciate the strong possibility that a woman's view of something will offer me an outlook I would never have imagined. The perspective of someone much older or younger will show me things I couldn't see myself. Even a child, sometimes, can reveal to me something I would never have learned if I hadn't listened.

In the company of the happy few we give and receive invaluable support and encouragement. We walk together cheering each other on.

Several times in this book I have written affectionately about some of my closest friends. In one chapter I mentioned Al Napolitano, who, just as I was finishing this book, went to be with Jesus.

There will be few memories in my life more precious than a long hike I took three years ago in the Swiss Alps with Al and two others. These were the three friends I spoke of at the beginning of this chapter.

The trail we took that day ended up to be far longer and more difficult than any of us had anticipated. It was about halfway along the pathway when we realized that Al, ten years older than the rest of us, had become seriously exhausted. There was a considerable distance yet to walk before we might find shelter, and I began to worry. Al had suffered from some serious heart problems a few years back, and I was concerned that we had unwittingly put him in a dangerous situation.

I suggested that the other two of our four-man group hike on ahead and find a place where we might spend the night. Al and I would continue walking, but at a much reduced pace.

I said to Al, "We'll take a hundred steps and rest. A hundred more steps and rest. If we are going uphill, you lead. If we're going downhill, I'll lead." We agreed and started on our way. Even with our sequence of a hundred steps and a rest, the way became more and more difficult for my friend.

Soon we were walking arm in arm, as if one of us was ushering the other down a church aisle. We prayed together, told stories to each other, and whispered words of encouragement. In this fashion we made our way forward until, as darkness fell, we reached the burghaus (mountain hotel) our friends had found for us. That walk brought me as close to the heart of another man as I have ever experienced.

Al went to be with the Lord just a few days ago. Asked to preside at his funeral, I made the account of our hike the theme of my sermon. I spoke of the stories we'd told one another, the prayers we prayed, the cheer we exchanged. You could tell that the entire congregation was captured by the drama of two men struggling together and reaching so deeply into each other's hearts.

Every one of us longs for relationships that are intimate and satisfying. What would it be like to be part of a happy few with whom there is freedom to acknowledge exhaustion or excitement, dreams or disappointment? Everyone wants just a few with whom they can walk arm in arm . . . a hundred steps and rest . . . a hundred steps and rest. In the resting is the lingering.

In the days just before Al left us for heaven, he and I sat and talked of our memories of that walk. Sitting close, we instinctively reached out our hands to one another, and in the grip of masculine affection, we talked about his illness and the strong possibility that he might not be with us much longer. "I'm ready to go if this is my time," he said.

When it came time to leave, I reminded Al of our hiking contract. "Al, every day of your illness is like a hundred steps. A hundred steps and rest, a hundred more and rest."

Al is the first to die among the happy few in my world. His was a resilient life.

Being part of a happy few means that each of us is held to higher standards of Christlikeness. Of what use are relationships if they do not call us to higher standards of Christian nobility?

There is a certain "niceness" to a friendship where I can be, as they say, *myself*. But what I really need are relationships in which I will be encouraged to become *better than* myself. *Myself* needs to grow a little each day. I don't want to be the *myself* I was yesterday. I want to be the *myself* that is developing each day to be more of a Christlike person.

Stanley Jones wrote of a moment when he penned a response to a letter from a harsh critic. Irritated by the letter, Jones gave vent to his feelings of hurt and defensiveness. He determined that he would be honest, to the point, respectful. But before he mailed his response, he offered his friends a chance to read it and to offer judgment.

When the unsent letter was returned to him, he saw that one of his happy few had written across the top "not sufficiently redemptive." Wise man that Jones was, he destroyed the letter. His friends had held him to a higher standard.

I have looked back across the years and asked myself, *who were the men and women I have appreciated the most?* And when I begin to name names, I discovered that almost every one of them is someone who was tough with me, who expected me to rise higher in character and conduct than I might have by myself.

In my files is a paper written in graduate school for a professor who encouraged my love of writing. The paper was so poor that the professor wrote on the last page, "If I were you, I would be ashamed to put my name on this."

When I see him and remind him of that remark made forty years ago, he groans. He wants to apologize for his harshness. But I tell him that it was what I needed. And I never write a manuscript today without asking myself along the way, *am I prepared to put my name on this writing?* This is the gift a friend offers when he or she challenges you to do your best.

When we are among the happy few, we make special things happen together that we could not have accomplished ourselves or done as well. It's called synergy.

I saw this happen on the Habitat for Humanity project in Hungary I mentioned earlier. About thirty people, almost all strangers, met at six-thirty on a Monday morning. A leader described our mission: take the materials delivered to the site, build a two-bedroom bungalow, and finish it by 4:00 PM on Friday so that a half hour later we could dedicate it and hand the keys over to the new owners. What intensified the drama was the fact that the soon-to-be owners were there to work with us. They had a nine-year-old daughter who had never lived in a home of her own, much less have her own bedroom.

We fairly attacked that pile of building materials. By the end of the first day, the house was almost fully framed. Each of us found ourselves so motivated that we had little interest in coffee breaks or mealtimes. When any project was finished, we immediately cried out, "Who needs me? Who needs me?" One hour I found myself leading a group on some assignment; the next hour I was following someone on his. None of us ever worked so hard, enjoyed the labor so thoroughly, and felt so motivated to reach our goal by the four o'clock hour on Friday.

We were a bunch of executives, researchers, computer programmers, clumsy pastors, and a few salespeople. But each day we became more and more a band of brothers (and sisters), "we happy few."

On Friday afternoon we reached our goal, and our team stood in a circle at the front door of the newly completed home. There were Germans, Americans, South Africans, Israelis, and Canadians. Throughout the week we had all tried to impress one another with our toughness and durability. But now we were wiping tears from our eyes as the keys were presented to our Hungarian friends and watched their daughter dance with joy as she anticipated moving into her own bedroom.

I want to add that among the happy few there should be genuine fun together. There is a couple with whom we have met every month for almost twenty years. The wives assure that dates for each month are in the calendar six months in advance, for we all live very busy lives. These occasions are filled with laughter, storytelling, and problem solving.

The pressure upon their lives—as with ours—often reaches a point of intolerability. There is the pressure of leadership, the self-doubt in the midst of tough decisions, the quest for courage when goals have to be met. But when the four of us meet, all of that pressure is suspended for a time, and we refresh one another. There is much laughter, the exchange of wisdom, the promise of prayer. A friendship that endures for twenty years cannot be measured or priced.

One more thought. A happy few with Jesus at the center may be the most important testimony that we are genuine followers of Christ. "By this all men will know that you are my disciples, [in the way] you love one another" (John 13:35).

Dare we forget this? Resilient people do not.

TWENTY-EIGHT

THERE ARE CERTAIN PEOPLE

In a 1987 book, *Jesus Man of Prayer*, Margaret Magdalene quotes Edward Farrell:

> Listening is rare. There are certain people we meet to whom we feel we can talk because they have such a deep capacity for hearing; not hearing words only but hearing us as a person. They enable us to talk on a level which we have never before reached. They enable us to be as we have never been before. We shall never truly know ourselves unless we find people who can listen, who can enable us to emerge, to come out of ourselves, to discover who we are. We cannot discover ourselves by ourselves.[1] (emphasis mine)

Listen again to Farrell: "*There are certain people . . .* [who] *enable us to be as we have never been before.*" The pathway to resilience requires that I fill my personal life with a very special set of relationships. Who makes up your happy few?

At the very center of the happy few in my world is my wife, Gail. Walking through life with her has been God's greatest gift to me.

I often think about this when I scrunch down next to her on the couch in our living room and we prepare to watch the evening news. I think of the depth of this relationship we share, one in which we are both heavily invested. Every few minutes, one of us moves, trying to get just a bit closer to the other. When the news is over, we often talk about the day. What happened? What did we learn? What challenges are we facing? Where is God speaking in the busyness? And I ask myself, *can it get any better than this?* You could call these lingering moments when, according to Edward Ferrell's thought, we get to know ourselves better through one another.

The journey Gail and I share together is scarred with a one-time deep hurt, but, far more significantly, it is decorated with countless delights and blessings. We know each other so well that we can usually finish each other's sentences, predict each other's choices, jump to meet the other's need before it is mentioned.

This is what intimacy is supposed to be. Originally, human beings were wired by the Creator to mirror the intimacy of the Trinity. "I pray," Jesus said to His heavenly Father, ". . . that all of them may be one, Father, just as you are in me and I am in you" (John 17:20–21). And we feel as if we taste just a bit of it.

No one will ever get close to what God intended. The original two people in the Bible were described as naked and unashamed (see Genesis 2:25). It suggests to me an openness that was so profound that both people could look to the core of the other's soul. Gail and I, and everyone else, have a long way to go before our level of intimacy could be described in such terms, but we are among those who make this our goal.

Resilient people seek this intimacy. They have come to appreciate the importance of traveling through life with a happy few, where there is a deep personal connectedness from which one derives continuous strength for the race. The search for a happy few is among their highest priorities.

In my thinking about the resilient life, I have pondered this matter of the happy few with great curiosity. Perhaps it is the result of coming out of a religious background where relationships were confusing and often unsatisfying. The memories of living in a contentious environment where people didn't take the time to understand one another and could not find ways to build in each others' lives have remained with me throughout my life. When I reached adulthood, I determined to know what it would take to make things different.

I've examined my relationships, with Gail, our extended family, our friends, and those with whom we share working relationships. I've tried to discern the key ingredients to all of those relationships. What is it that I can give? And what is it that I need?

I have framed my search for the happy few in the form of questions. I offer you the ones that have come to mean the most to me.

———

I have asked myself, *who coaches you?* Coaching may be the new buzzword to replace *disciple, mentor,* and *teacher.* I like it because it envisions that older, wiser, more experienced person who stands on the sideline of one's life and watches with a big picture in mind. A coach does not try to run the race for his athletes. But the coach certainly sets the standard for the race and makes a judgment on the performance.

I started this book with the description of my ideal of a coach: Marvin Goldberg. He was the first of several in my life.

I can't imagine life without a coach, that person who represents the greatest possibility of stability and certainty in the human experience. The coach is one whose word and whose opinion you trust. This is the person who gives you the truest picture of yourself. And, finally, the coach is the one who may have the best view of what you're capable of becoming.

I have an appreciative memory of one of my coaches, a man by the name of Chet Amsden, who is now with Jesus. When I was given the privilege of being pastor to a New England congregation that called itself Grace Chapel, Chet Amsden was the chairman of the board of elders, the governing group of the congregation. Professionally, Amsden was a sales representative for the Xerox Corporation, but I think he secretly worked for Grace Chapel.

I was a young thirty-two-year-old when I stepped into congregational life in Lexington, Massachusetts, and I needed a coach— someone who could show me around, point out the landmines of organizational life, shake a disapproving finger when I began to expose signs of immaturity.

Chet Amsden was the kind of man who would hand you a box of breath mints when you needed them as you approached people in need of prayer. He could prepare you with the kind of questions that made you come to board meetings fully prepared. And he wasn't above challenging the logic of a sermon if he felt it needed a bit more "beef." But beyond all that, he was also the first cheerleader when I did something right. I was never confused about where I stood with the Grace Chapel congregation as long as Chet Amsden was my coach.

Who would want to walk through life without the discipline of a man or woman like that? Can such be found? I must tell you that I have never found it problematic to locate one. Coaches and teachable people find one another. Anyone with questions will soon find people with answers.

Abraham Joshua Heschel wrote, "What we need more than anything else is not text-books but text-people. It is the personality of the teacher which is the text that the pupils read; the text they will never forget."[2]

Moses coached Joshua for the better part of forty years. "Write these things down," God once said to Moses, "so that he'll have what he needs after you're gone" (my paraphrase). And that's the first person I seek among my happy few: the "old guy" who cares where I'm headed. But come to think of it . . . I am now, more or less, the "old guy" for a few of those who are in search of a coach. This is very sobering to me.

———

Who stretches your mind? Among my happy few are a few thinkers, men and women who are not afraid to poke and prod into my mind with different viewpoints than I have. They challenge my politics, my theology, my self-confidence about life-direction, my ways of leading, the guiding ideas of my life. They provide me with book titles and magazine articles; they call world events to my attention; they introduce me to topics I didn't even know existed. And they often make me wince as they expose the many faces of my ignorance . . . which is quite OK.

Just as Marvin Goldberg once pushed me in the development of my body, these mind stretchers push me in the growth of my thinking. They will not let me easily get away with intellectual superficiality.

———

Who listens to and encourages your dreams? A distinctive quality of the human being is in the ability to imagine possibilities, to think about what could be tomorrow. But that is done best in the company of friends who are willing to listen.

Dreams are not like intellectual propositions which must be proven. Dreams are the work of a visionary; they're wild, out-of-the-box, frequently awful, occasionally good. I have been a dreamer all of my life. Too much the dreamer, one of my teachers often said. As the romantic dreamer, I experienced a lot of derisive laughter from individuals who had no patience with people who built castles in the air.

I recall the snickers that arose the first time I tried reading a piece of creative writing. To be sure, it deserved the ridicule. But derision is what defeats so many who dare to think that there are gifts and visions and opportunities down the line that no one has yet thought of.

That's why it's important to have a few people in one's life who listen to the dreams and point out where the possibilities lie.

I am convinced that the first thing that caused me to fall in love with Gail was that she listened to my dreams. Those whom I'd known in dating relationships before she entered my life often rolled their eyes when I dared to talk about tomorrow and my aspirations. They made it clear that they had doubts that I would ever amount to much. But when Gail and I talked, I heard her say, "I can see how that could happen . . . That sounds terrific. God could really bless that." And I loved her for it.

"Your dreams are pretty expensive," Gail would say occasionally. But it was affectionate kidding. I knew she was aboard, that she saw in all of those crazy dreams of mine the possibility of a life of ministry. And together we have pursued those dreams (and many more) ever since.

———

When forming a happy few, one might want to ask, who will protect you? This is the friend who will not let others slander or misrepresent you. When there is a need for an advocate, one who will make sure that others hear what you are about, the protector is the person who will make sure that the truth is told.

In the Bible, Barnabas turned out to be that kind of a person. When the Christians in Jerusalem wanted to have nothing to do with the newly converted Saul of Tarsus, it was Barnabas who acted as his advocate. He was the one who brought Saul into the Christian movement with the apparent assurance that he would be responsible for him.

When the newly minted church at Antioch needed pastoral leadership, it was Barnabas who went off to Saul's home city of Tarsus, found him and brought him back, and put him in the seat of pastoral influence. Because of Barnabas's interest, a congregation grew.

And when Barnabas's nephew, John Mark, failed the test on the very first missionary journey that Saul (Paul) and Barnabas took, it was Barnabas who later stood up for the young man and demanded that he be given a second chance.

Barnabas is the kind of friend I am talking about. Whether it was Saul of Tarsus, the Antiochean congregation, or John Mark, Barnabas was always looking out for their best interests.

In one of his first books, *Genesse Diary*,[3] Henry Nouwen recounted working in the bakery of the monastery of the Abbey of the Genesee. Suddenly, he said, one of the monks with whom he was working turned off the machine. He had heard a noise indicating to him that a stone was among the raisins. It had to be found, he insisted, because it could have disastrous implications if someone chewed a piece of bread and broke a tooth.

It seemed impossible, Nouwen said, to find a stone that small among the millions of raisins in the bathtublike container. But the monks were insistent. "We have to push those [raisins] through again until we find that stone."

The raisins were pushed through again and then suddenly every one heard a click. A monk reached in among the raisins and pulled out a small purple-blue stone.

In some small way this event meant a lot to me. Yesterday I was carrying granite rocks out of the river. Today we were looking for a small stone among millions of raisins. I was impressed, not only by Theodore's alertness, but even more by his determination to find it and take no risks. He really is a careful diagnostician . . .

And I thought about purity and purification. Even the small stone that looks like all these good-tasting raisins has to be taken out. I can't even notice my own little sins, but it offers me consolation to know that someone will keep a careful watch on me and stop the machine when he hears a stone between the raisins. That really is care.[4]

———

Among those who populate your happy few, *who are those who share your tears?*

Three of the Gospel writers relate the story of Mary of Bethany who, a night or two before Jesus was arrested and crucified, poured expensive perfume on His feet and head. It appears that everyone else in the room, including the disciples, was disgusted. "Why this waste?" Judas asked, probably with his own agenda in mind.

My wife has often pointed out to me that Mary was the only person in the room that understood what Jesus was going through. Somehow she had intuited His increased tension and inner distress as He came closer and closer to the awful hour. She alone shared His tears.

And Jesus was aware that she was aware. "She poured perfume on my body beforehand to prepare for my burial," He said (Mark 14:8). Throughout that final week there was not one man who ever had the slightest idea that Jesus was in the battle of His life. They never picked up on it! Mary did.

Resilient people are never to be complainers or whiners. Yet there are still tears to be shed over the tough issues of life. Who is close enough to us to pick up the themes and sense the moment when tears must be shared? While there are times when one is in need of someone who can offer a pep talk, a back pat, or a shot in the arm, there are also times when one needs to be encouraged to lie low for a while, to let the tears flow. Who does that for you?

I appreciate the fact that God seems to have done this for Elijah in his exhausted moments in the wilderness. He had stood tall on the top of a mountain as he humiliated the priests of Baal, and an entire nation had witnessed the explosive power of God.

We make a lot out of his capitulation to the threats of Queen Jezebel without ever realizing that the man must have been almost a basket case when he finished at the top of the mountain. Truth is, he desperately needed that downtime in the wilderness. And whether or not he said all the right things is less important than the fact that God gave him space and saw to it that he got food, drink, and sleep. Only then did God teach him a lesson or two.

———

Then one must ask, *who rebukes you?* Who is there in one's bevy of relationships who loves enough to speak correctively?

In her biography of Oliver Wendell Holmes, Elizabeth Drinker Bowen records one of the justice's favorite stories of the orphan who often stuck out his tongue at the emperor whenever he passed by. The kid drove the emperor mad. There must "always be someone to remind you that your crown isn't on straight."

In the kind of English language used in 1722, Jonathan Edwards wrote in his journal:

Considering that by-standers always espy some faults which we don't see ourselves, or at last are not so fully sensible of:

there are many secret workings of corruption which escape our sight, and others only are sensible of: resolved, therefore, that I will, if I can by any convenient means, learn what faults others find in me, or what things they see in me, that appear anyway blame-worthy, unlovely or unbecoming.[5]

Not many years after (in 1783, to be exact) Charles Simeon wrote to his friend Henry Venn about a rebuke he'd received from a fellow pastor. Simeon had been challenged about the sloppiness of his sermon, and he took the reprimand rather well. To Venn he wrote:

What a blessing—an inestimable blessing is it to have a faithful friend! Satan is ready enough to point out whatever good we have; but it is only a faithful friend that will screen that from your sight, and show you your deficiencies. Our great apostasy seems to consist primarily in making a god of self; and he is the most valuable friend who will draw us most from self-seeking—self-pleasing—and self-dependence, and help us to restore to God the authority we have robbed him of.[6]

In other places I have written of the memorable rebukes that have been aimed in my direction. None so powerful, however, as the ones that have come from Gail. "God has given you a powerful gift in Gail," said the man who had introduced me to her. "She will teach you many things you need to know if you are willing to listen to her. Don't be like so many men who cannot listen to and learn from those closest to them." Most of the time, I have indeed listened and profited. When I didn't, I lost.

———

Who among your happy few plays with you? Does this seem to be an innocuous question in a somewhat serious book about the resilient life? Trust me: it is a worthy question, and it must be separated out and highlighted. To play! The root word for the English word *play* has mostly to do with learning. Good play is a learning experience.

Play for two people I know in their midsixties is a good movie, a dinner out, a walk in the mountains, a favorite TV show, making love. It is agreeing to a moment in the day when all work will come to an end, when conversation will not include work issues, and when refreshment of body and soul is the chief priority.

As I said in a previous chapter, play almost went out of our lives when our children left home to seek their own futures. For years we stood on the sidelines and watched them play their games, and cheered. We savored the time about the dinner table each night when the family gathered to eat and talk. We loved the friends they brought home to hang out for an evening. Then, suddenly, it all stopped, and we didn't realize that we'd have to learn to play in a different way all over again.

We love the precious moments when we gather with our friends for a movie, a concert, an overnight to a neighboring city. The exchanges of humorous cards, the e-mail traffic, the phone calls, all part of connections that bring joy and lightness to what could otherwise be a heavy, heavy life.

It took us time to learn these new ways. And there are times when we still struggle because there is so much to do and so little time. We must not let the seriousness of life override the need for recreation (a word more meaningful when it is properly hyphenated, re-creation).

———

But there is one final question that must be asked as we examine the pieces of a solidarity-based relationship. Among your happy few, *who is it that seeks after God with you?*

We who think of ourselves as "Bible people" need to evaluate our relationships and assure ourselves that spiritual pursuits are a part of life together. Praying, growing, serving together.

I struggled with this as a younger man. Like many, I felt uncomfortable, kind of sheepish when it came to inviting my wife or my friends to a life of prayer. Perhaps it had something to do with my pride as a man. I didn't do any better with the men I knew. Those closest to me were all confessing Christians. We conducted ourselves in a fashion that could be considered Christian. But it was difficult to talk of our faith in a personal way. It was almost as if God was the elephant in the room that no one knew how to talk about.

Praying together as a married couple or among friends was difficult then. Probably because prayer is an acknowledgment of dependence and weakness, and we feel very self-conscious when prayer is invited into personal relationships. Most men struggle in using the traditional prayer vocabulary. The words commonly used in most acceptable prayers are simply not spoken in everyday language. Beyond that, men are reluctant to pray for fear that it opens up parts of the inner self that one wants to keep closed.

The low moments in my life solved this problem for me, because there came times when I could not mask my weaknesses and pretend that I was a well-put-together man. My weaknesses confessed themselves for me, and it was time to turn to the most important person in my world (Gail) and to my friends and say, "I need prayer."

Today in our marriage, our daily exchanges in insights, journal entries, prayers, and senses of God's purpose are, for us, a normal part of our lives together. Gone is the self-consciousness, the fear of awkwardness, the worry that I might not appear to be as mature as I ought to be.

When the group with whom we meet monthly reaches the hour

when we know we must embrace and say good-bye, we enter into the presence of the Father. The evening's conversation has told us all we need to know about each other's updated stories. We know whose grandchildren need prayer, who's on his way to see a doctor, who's headed into a challenging project for the kingdom. We know who's facing a deadline, who's in need of wisdom, who's headed for a trip. And we pray *fervently* for one another. We lift one another to God.

"*There are certain people . . .* [who] *enable us to be as we have never been before,*" writes Edward Farrell. These are the happy few. And in their company, we find resilience.

A LETTER I WISH I'D WRITTEN

Dear Marvin,

I've written a book that sort of makes you into a hero . . . my hero anyway. I know you well enough that, if you could, you would make me go back and expunge all references to you and your role in my life. You never were a man who was comfortable in the spotlight. All your achievements were in the lives of other people.

But St. Paul told us to take note of those who live godly lives and to study them. This is my way of doing that, Marvin.

When I first met you in the fall of 1954, I was a boy barely out of puberty. When I said good-bye to you in June of 1957, I was on my way to manhood. In our first meeting, I called you "sir," and after I ran my last race for you, you invited me to call you Marvin.

I find that reminiscent of the day Jesus said to His disciples, "I no longer call you servants, because a servant does not know his master's business. Instead, I have called you friends, for everything that I learned from my Father I have made known to you" (John 15:15). Thank you, Marvin, for training me as a runner and then making me a friend.

It has taken me fifty years, Marvin, to realize that my view of how to live life was crystallized on the Stony Brook track and cross-country course where you built your teams. I can't imagine there has been a day since the first time I met you at the white bulletin board that I haven't drawn upon the principles learned in those days.

Now I know that my passion to be a resilient man came from you. You were the one who was always pointing out that it was in the second half of the race that champions show what they're made of. You loved and respected the athlete who ran strong to the tape.

Now I am well into the second half of life's race, and I have come to believe that this is the time for someone like myself to do his best work for the kingdom and to show the strongest evidence of Christ's character in life. You taught me to think that way, Marvin.

Thank you for teaching me the value of the big picture, the importance of having an overarching direction in life that presumably comes from God call.

Thank you for impressing upon me the importance of not living in the past, except to drain it for its lessons and experiences.

And thanks for the constant emphasis on self-discipline and for making it clear that if I would push myself, I would not only be an athlete, but also a person God could use as He filled me with His Spirit.

Finally, Marvin, thank you for making sure that I understood the strength-giving nature of a team—a happy few, a band of brothers and sisters.

Now that you're in heaven, Marvin, I am unable to come to where you are and tell you how much your place in my life has meant. But I can write and tell stories about your influence in my life and hope that it makes a difference in the lives of those who are kind enough to read this book. And when I do that, I will always say in conclusion, you were one of the most resilient men I ever knew.

I thank God for you, sir,

Gordie

NOTES

CHAPTER 2

1. E. Stanley Jones, *A Song of Ascents* (Abingdon Press, 1968), 20.

CHAPTER 3

1. Oswald Chambers, *Leagues of Light: Diary of Oswald Chambers 1915–1917* (Louisville, KY: Operation Appreciation Ministries, Inc.).
2. Scott Turrow, *The Laws of Our Fathers* (New York: Warner Books, 1996).
3. Source text unknown.

CHAPTER 6

1. Lewis Carroll, *Alice's Adventures in Wonderland*, and *Through the Looking Glass* (New York: Signet).
2. M. Basis Pennington, *Thomas Merton: Brother Monk* (Harper & Row, 1987).
3. Stephen Ambrose, *Nothing Like It in the World* (New York: Simon & Schuster, 2001).
4. Ibid., 117.

CHAPTER 7

1. Jon Dean, *Blind Ambition* (Simon & Schuster, 1976).

CHAPTER 8

1. Alan Jones, *Soul Making* (Harper & Row, 1985), 12.
2. Erwin McManus, *Seizing Your Divine Moment* (Nashville: Nelson Books, 2003).
3. From the writings of St. Therese of Lisieux.
4. Quoted by Jay Kessler, *Growing* (out of print), 41.

CHAPTER 12

1. David Abshire, *The Character of George Washington*. The speech from which this quote was taken was found at www.thepresidency.org.

CHAPTER 13

1. James MacGregor Burns, *Leadership* (New York: HarperCollins, 1979).

CHAPTER 15
1. John Claypool, *The Preaching Event* (Waco, TX: Word Publishers, 1980).

CHAPTER 18
1. Neal Bascomb, *The Perfect Mile* (Houghton Mifflin, 2004).
2. Thomas Merton, *New Seeds of Contemplation* (New York: New Directions, 1972).
3. Elton Trueblood, *The Company of the Committed* (HarperCollins, 1979).
4. Bill Toomey, www.billtoomey.com

CHAPTER 20
1. Neil Bascomb, *The Perfect Mile* (Houghton Mifflin), 279.

CHAPTER 21
1. Cited by Os Guinness in the Trinity Forum Curriculum on character, *When No One Sees*.

CHAPTER 22
1. William Barclay, James: Daily Bible Study Series (Philadelphia: Westminster).

CHAPTER 23
1. Source unknown.
2. John Stott, *Alive to God* (out of print).
3. Clarence Hall, *Samuel Logan Brengle: Portrait of a Prophet* (Chicago: Salvation Army Supply and Purchasing Department,1933).
4. Frances Hesselbein, Marshall Goldsmith, Richard Beckhard, and Richard Schubert, *The Community of the Future* (Jossey-Bass, 1998).

CHAPTER 24
1. John Battersby Harford and Frederick Charles MacDonald, *Handley Carr Glyn Moule: Bishop of Durham* (Hodder and Stroughton, 1922).
2. Brother Lawrence, *Practicing the Presence of God* (Nashville: Thomas Nelson, 1982).
3. Paul Sangster, *Doctor Sangster* (Epworth, 1962).

CHAPTER 25
1. "If You Know the Lord."
2. Malcolm Gladwell, *The Tipping Point* (Little, Brown, 2000).

CHAPTER 26

1. Henri J.M. Nouwen, *In the Name of Jesus* (Crossroad, 1989), 60.
2. M. Basil Pennington, *Thomas Merton: Brother Monk* (Harper & Row, 1987).

CHAPTER 27

1. Nelson Mandela, *Long Walk to Freedom* (Little, Brown, and Company, 1994).

CHAPTER 28

1. Margaret Magdalene, *Jesus, Man of Prayer* (Eagle Publishing, 1999).
2. Marvin Wilson, *Our Father Abraham* (Grand Rapids: Eerdmans, 1989), 280.
3. Henri J. M. Nouwen, *The Genesee Diary* (Doubleday, 1966).
4. *Ibid.*, 16.
5. Jonathan Edwards, *Resolutions*.
6. William Carus, *Memoirs of the Life of Rev. Charles Simeon* (NY: Robert Carter Publisher, 1848).

ABOUT THE AUTHOR

Gordon MacDonald has been a pastor and author for more than forty years. Presently he serves as editor-at-large for *Leadership Journal* and as chairman of World Relief. His most recent books include *The Life God Blesses, Renewing Your Spiritual Passion, Rebuilding Your Broken World,* the best-seller *Ordering Your Private World,* and *When Men Think Private Thoughts.* MacDonald can often be found hiking the mountains of New England or Switzerland with his wife, Gail, or their five grandchildren.

Also from Gordon MacDonald…

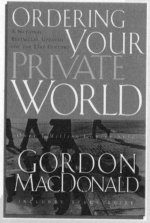

ISBN: 0-7852-6381-0

Newly revised, this popular bestseller on organizing our inner, spiritual world leads to an opportunity for a deeper experience with God and an understanding of our mission in serving Him.

Ordering Your Private World is phenomenal, selling over 1 million copies upon its original release in 1984. With revisions and new material, it is ever more timely to readers. Never admitting to have it all together, but rather using his own personal struggle as a way for readers to relate to his principles, Gordon MacDonald's classic book invites readers to bring order to their personal life by inviting God's control over every segment of their lives. His premise is that if the private world of a person is in order, it will be because they are convinced that the inner world of the spiritual must govern the outer world of activity.

The author of *Ordering Your Private World* helps men and women breathe new vitality into their faith and grow beyond the status quo to find fresh adventure and joy in life.

Mid-Course Correction offers hope not only for those who have experienced defeat and disappointment in their lives, but also for those who have been "successful" yet yearn for something more. MacDonald focuses on making choices that lead to personal transformation, significant communal relationships, practical service in the kingdom of God, and a revitalized life of faith and worship.

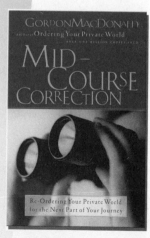

ISBN: 0-7852-6762-X